Bishop Larry Jackson

The True Value of a Woman

"God Designed You for Greatness"

Breastplate Prayer Publications

The True Value of a Woman

by Bishop Larry Jackson

Copyright © 2013

Breastplate Prayer Publications

Distributed by Frontliners Ministries

3715 Ridge Road

Charlotte, NC 28262

Cover Design: Maier Tudor

Editor: Valerie Hunt

Printed in the United States of America

ISBN: 0-9857687-4-6

Contents

Kathy Foster

May the Blessings of
God be in
your life

Bishop Larry Jack

Forward

This is wisdom you'll wish you had ten years ago! There are not many books that have the power to position you to fulfill your God-given purpose like Bishop Larry Jackson's, *True Value of a Woman*. Larry Jackson is one of the most incredible and inspiring Bible teachers on the planet. He's a man who walks daily with honor and integrity. As a faithful husband and loving father of five daughters, he has plenty of opportunity to practice what he preaches. Reading this book is a life-changing experience. You'll never be the same!

John Aitken, Senior Pastor
Faith Center of Paducah

True Value of a Woman is the single most important book I've read in the last decade on the position of a woman in the Kingdom of God. Bishop Jackson offers fresh clarity on how God has empowered ladies to thrive in their role as half of the supernatural partnership between a man and woman. He gets inside our hearts and articulates what we've long suspected since the Garden about our place on the planet. If you don't read any other book on the Creator's perfect design for a woman of worth, read this one!

Sarah Adams

While contemplating all the truths I discovered in this book, the one word that I keep hearing was Restoration. Reading this book has restored power, identity, and honor to every woman. Buckle your seats as Bishop Jackson outlines the journey for entering into a divine partnership with The Father; a partnership which impacts generations and unearths the treasure within.

Tia Boone

Since 1993, it has been my fortunate privilege to spend a tremendous amount of time with Bishop Jackson. I have been able to travel with him all across the nation. I have seen him minister the word of God with great inspiration and encouragement to thousands of people. I have seen him stand in meetings before five people as well as five thousand people and the message has always been intense and non-compromising regardless of the size of the audience. Bishop Jackson is a tremendous man of God! I really believe that He is one of God's best kept secrets. Anyone that ever gets to spend time with him is always amazed by his genuine love and compassion for people.

Bishop Jackson is spiritual father to me as well as several men of God. He absolutely has a father's heart. He has a heart is to see all of the sons and daughters to go further and be more successful than himself. I have seen from a firsthand experience that he absolutely loves his wife "like Christ loves the church" and he has raised all five of his daughters in the "fear and admonition of the Lord."

With "True Value of a Woman", Bishop Jackson truly unfolds to women how to take their rightful place in God. Through "True Value of a Woman", women get to see from a biblical perspective that they are not an afterthought but that God was very "hands on" in their creation and that women will play and are playing an indispensable role in the overall plan of God. The women that have attended the "True Value of A woman" seminars all leave encouraged and motivated to do more for Christ, because these women know that God truly values them.

Pressing Towards the Mark,
Pastor Paul Blue
Senior Pastor, Clinton International Church

The published works of Bishop Larry Jackson have been known to impact readers within and without the Body of Christ, with depths of revelatory exactness for some time. Each of his books has brought operative realities to the life encounters of those who have taken the time to read.

Bishop Jackson's latest endeavor, "The True Value of a Woman", is expected to match, if not excel, the same powerful impact as his previous works.

"The True Value of a Woman" is an obtainable treasure to the women that will investigate its pages. Every woman who has struggled with negative issues in their personal lives; every woman who has struggled with their true identity and God's established purpose will welcome the adventure. Although the book was written about the woman, to bring clarity to the woman, it is not just for the woman. This is a must read for the husbands, fathers, brothers, sons, and others whom God has used to honor the women in their lives. Expect to be enlightened and encouraged by this anointed work from Bishop Larry Jackson.

Pastor Diane Chappelle
Ruth Chapel A.M.E. Church
Vision of Hope Ministries, Spiritual Advisor

Dedication

This book, as are all of my books, is dedicated to my wife Joanndra, who has allowed me a place in her life for 28 years and has helped me accomplish the things given me by our Lord! Thank you honey from the bottom of my heart!

To my five daughters; it is a blessing to be involved in your lives. Each of you has qualities that I speak to people about across the church landscape. It is a wonderful thing that you call me father.

To my mother, it was because you showed me how a woman could be tender and strong at the same time that helped to mold my opinion about the women in my life. Thank you for the insight that you gave me it will forever be honored.

To each of my spiritual daughters who also call me dad it is a joy that you see something in me that you want to be connected to. Each of you has special places in my heart.

To the many women in my church that serve in the vision of God and allow me to pastor you, thanks for your love and support!

To Annette Williams, thank you for your patience and support through this and many other projects.

Your willingness to learn new things to see the Kingdom of God advanced is special to me.

To every woman who has decided to walk in the freedom and anointing that our Lord has provided, thank you for your example!

Preface

One of the television shows that I enjoyed watching during my childhood was the "The Beverly Hillbillies." Because I watched the program daily, it wasn't long before the words of the theme song became a part of my memory.

I will come back to the show in just a minute. Over the last 17 years I have been vitally involved in the Men's Movement that has help to sharpen and increase scores of men across North America.

My own men's ministry "Frontliners Men's Ministry" was birthed in 1999 and is still functioning today in several church communities across America. Men frequently approach me as I travel to report how our Lord helped change their lives through a particular message that I've spoken.

Father God has given me a unique way to minister to men and it's a wonderful thing to watch a man turn from sin to follow Jesus Christ our Lord!

The other place I've focused during this time is to help city leaders understand how to work together for the Kingdom advancement. That many of these leaders are men kept my main focus on men and the issues facing their lives.

During my years working with Promise Keepers Men's Ministry, one of my primary messages was to men concerning marriage. The goal of the messages were to teach men how to lead their wives into the face of Almighty God and how to serve them as Christ serves and loves the church.

In my role as a local Pastor, I understand how important it is to have strong marriages and families for the overall stability of the church. Because marriage is under great attack today from the prevailing culture, information that helps couples understand their roles and responsibilities to each other is greatly needed.

For this reason, we developed a marriage class that meets twice a month before the Sunday morning service and it is a great success. It is one of the best attended classes at the church and it always has a great deal of excitement surrounding it.

The revelation that God gave me concerning women began to free the hearts and minds of the women attending the classes. They indicated that all of the women in our church should know what they were learning and asked if I would have a special meeting to share that information.

Our church has a dynamic women's ministry, "Women of Zion," overseen by my wife. The Women of Zion ministry is connected to our

Fellowship of International Churches organizational women's ministry, "Kingmakers," under the leadership of Bishop Wellington Boone, who has written a book by the same title.

For these reasons, I didn't want to have another meeting that would compete with these two vehicles that were doing just fine in my estimation. But the women in the class wouldn't let it go so I finally gave in and told them if they pulled it together I would do it.

With virtually no advertisement, only word of mouth and a short last minute You Tube video, our church was full of women from all across the city.

During the time I was preparing for the one day meeting, something came alive in my heart and I realized that God was the one setting all of this up, not the women, which takes me back to The Beverly Hillbillies television program.

In the theme song, Jed Clampett sings that he "...was shooting at some food and up from the ground came a bubblin' crude. Oil that is, black gold, Texas tea." He was trying to meet one small need and an entirely different and much larger need was supplied!

That is how I feel about the information in this book. It wasn't what I was looking for, but it is what

God gave to meet the need of so many women and even men. The reports we have received from those attending the meeting as well as those who have listened to the recorded messages have been tremendous.

Men have listened and indicated that they had no idea that God has valued women in the way He has. I have shared the message in men's meetings and they have actually run to my product table to purchase the recordings that were taught to the women.

It is my prayer that the information in this book will help you in the same way. So now it is your time to tap your well of oil that is waiting deep down inside of you. If you are a woman reading this book, please understand that God has never made any invaluable person or thing, so start thinking of yourself like He sees you!

God Bless!

Introduction

This book is written from a completely different perspective than other material of its kind. When this subject is taught in conferences and churches, I guarantee that the audience will hear me say things that neither their mother nor any other woman in their lives has shared with them.

As a father, I understand the way most fathers love their daughters and want the very best for them. It is a father's heart to teach his daughter how to avoid the traps that can be set by men who have their own agenda at heart. Fathers have expressed their gratefulness for the principled information shared in this book that will help them with their children.

We have heard from women and men who testify how much the True Value principle helped them instruct their sons and daughters about a woman's value. Most people tell us that they have never heard much of this information. There were several women in the first meeting of "The True Value of a Woman," whose ages ranged from 60 to 75 that indicated they had never heard this information, and especially not from a man.

Now, please believe me that I am not reaching over my shoulder attempting to pat myself on the back.
One thing is sure: when someone makes a claim like the one above it captures the attention of the audience it is directed towards. But this isn't meant as a shock and awe

statement designed just to grab attention at the start of a book.

These things have actually happened to even my surprise! Everything discussed has its foundation in the word of God. God has given me these insights over the last 25 years as I prayed for and spent time focusing my attention on the women in my life. I will discuss my family more later, but for now know that it consists of a wonderful wife I have been married to for 28 years and 5 lovely daughters whose lives have helped to form much of the natural understanding I discovered.

Before having children, I prayed to have daughters who would embrace the standard of God set forth by the word of God, but I had no idea that He would give me this type of revelation concerning them. In addition to my natural daughters, God has placed in my life many spiritual daughters, all of whom believe they are number one and have more favor with me than any of the others! Therefore it is important that I understand how to increase the happiness and prosperity of the women in my life.

A man who understands the value of a woman will understand her uniqueness, while doing everything in his power to help her increase both spiritually and naturally. Herein is one of the problems in the society: we have lost the secure man who is not threatened by the success of a woman. As you will see, God designed men and women to be successful in every area of their lives. When this is understood they can then become successful together instead working against each other.

Women are such awesome creatures, who were created to be God's crowning seal of creation. Because of the fall, the woman lost her special place and many of the original purposes for her life have gone unrealized, or in many cases, completely overlooked!

My main focus in writing this book is to help women realize who they are and how special they are to God and should be to man. In today's culture, the information concerning a woman's value and how much God cares for her can be more than enough to accomplish my earlier claims. But there is so much that has not been fully explored by the church concerning women that a book this size could never include it all.

After making these claims I realize that there are still church organizations that have a very low opinion about women and their role in and outside of the church. They have developed wrong perspectives about the role of women in the church; this is due to them not investigating the New Covenant as a completely new relationship to God that even surpasses the relationship of Adam and Mrs. Adam.

There is no wonder many professional women don't want to submit to the church leadership who doesn't see them as important when the world system is fully embracing their abilities and achievements. When I read the bible and study the New Covenant, it is clear that God restored all that was lost in Adam's sin, which would also include the woman's role in the disobedience.

If she is restored with everything else that was corrupted by Adam's sin, then it is time to go back to God's original intent for her existence and allow her to function the way He designed. Women must be told and begin to operate as Women of God and things that once seemed difficult to accomplish will become easier because things will be in proper alignment.

The world is waiting and watching, so let's get busy putting in place this lost principle of how truly valuable women are and how important their position is to creation!

May God bless you, and happy reading!

Section 1: The Foundation

Vision:

Empowering Women through clarity about who they really are, commitment to God, connection to each other and community involvement!

Mission:

Understand how God sees you. Learn how to reach and influence men. Understand your true position.

Chapter 1: The Beginning

*You don't love a woman
because she is beautiful, but is she
beautiful because you love her?*

~Unknown

The subject matter found in this book has the ability to establish new foundations in the lives of the reader while destroying old strongholds which can keep many women and men from experiencing God's best for their lives. For this reason all of the opinions will be firmly based upon the Bible (Word of God) as the book's primary source. When other research materials are referenced they will all be used to strengthen a biblical view. Whenever the word of God is used to investigate any subject it is important to discover the first time it was presented or mentioned in the Bible. This is the original place the subject is discussed or the person is introduced and it will give a clear picture to what is in the heart of God concerning the subject matter or person.

I will use this first mention principle many times in this book to help establish a proper foundation and framework for this extremely important subject. It is my prayer that every woman reading this book will better understand who they are and begin to function accordingly. I pray a new standard will be developed and women will begin to see themselves the way God intends. When this happens men will again celebrate and defend our women who are now being used in so many demeaning ways in today's culture. It is also my prayer that men reading this book who have a poor understanding and even a dismissive mindset about the value of women will gain insight that helps renew their hearts and understanding. Can someone say, "Amen?"

In Our Image

In the Genesis account of creation the bible points out that man was created on the sixth day, but that God communicated with the man and the woman before their physical creation. Since Genesis is the first book of the bible, it is easy to see that things found in it are established in the first mention principle. Reading the book of Genesis will help establish an understanding about mankind (man and woman) and what plans God had for them from the beginning.

Apparent immediately is the fact that creation was designed to respond to man and woman and not vice versa. It is also obvious that men and women are both special in the heart of the Godhead even above the rest of the creation and that they are created to enjoy the works of God's hand.

In Genesis 1:26 the bibles reads, *And God said, Let us make man in our image . . .*

The words "us" and "our" is the Hebrew word *Elohim,* which is the plural form of God. It refers to the True God of Majesty, the complete Godhead- Father, Son and Holy Spirit, and is used over two thousand times in the bible. The whole existence of God is in full agreement that mankind will be created in the image of God.

The word for "image" is the Hebrew word *tselem* meaning image, form, appearance, or semblance. We are all created in God's image.

When you consider that man is created in God's image it is very humbling especially when you understand that no other creature was given this honor. None of the animals were given God's appearance, His attributes, or His abilities like mankind was given. There are organizations and people who attempt to place animals on the same level as humans but this isn't found biblically.

The truth is that animals are all created beings but they are not created in God's image. It is a great thing to love animals and even protect them from abuse, but they should never be placed on the same level as mankind because they were placed under the authority of man.

A new importance must be given to the fact that man is formed in the image of God and how very special this is in the sight of God. The foundation for everything that mankind is to accomplish on this earth has to do with the fact they (man and woman) are functioning from God's image. A major problem facing people today is that they have forgotten or even debate the fact of being created in God's image.

There is no debate in the bible and for women to be seen the way God intended, a proper foundation concerning creation is a must. Therefore, the remainder of this book will work from the premise that God is our creator and we are all created in His image.

The remainder of the verse in Genesis 1:26 reads:

Then God said,

"... and let them have dominion over the fish of the sea, and over the fowl of the air, and over the cattle, and over all the earth, and over every creeping thing that creepeth upon the earth.

Notice God says let "them," He's not speaking exclusively about the man. He's declaring that both the man and the woman, "them", would function in harmony with the Godhead to oversee the earth. When God makes this proclamation, there is no distinction between them, no separation of any kind. The *Elohim* is releasing to the man and woman their authority to rule over the creation.

Every part of the creation account is submitted under the authority of the man and woman which can also cause your head to hurt when sitting and considering this amazing responsibility. But never the less they had it and were created with the ability to handle it all.

And He (God) says,

*Genesis 1:27 So God created man in his own image, in the image of God created he him; male and female created he **them**.*

The Genesis account reveals God's design for the man and woman at the moment of their creation and it would appear that they were created before being formed in the natural. They commune with God In the spiritual or unseen realm *before* they were created in the natural visible realm. It is in the spiritual realm where true authority can be received and understood.

That the woman wasn't immediately created when God comes down to fashion the man could suggest to some that the woman wasn't as important or equal to the man. But it was already established that the man and woman would have dominion over the works of God's hand and the order of their physical bodily creation didn't change that fact.

This principle is known as the original intent of God's heart for mankind. The first couple was designed to operate as one person with complete and unbroken relationship with their creator. Many have tried to determine why God created the man first if He wasn't saying that man was better than the woman.

The reason for God bringing the man on the scene first was not because he was better than the woman but for the purpose of spiritual order. The spiritual order will become even more apparent when we investigate their responsibility in the garden beyond being fruitful, multiplying and replenishing the earth. Always keep in mind that God saw the man and woman as one even though they were created at different times.

It Is All About Them

In Genesis Chapter 1 each time man and woman are referenced it is together; there is never a time where they are viewed as two separate beings.

*Genesis 1:28 And God blessed **them**, and God said unto **them**, Be fruitful, and multiply, and replenish the earth, and subdue it*

They are blessed together and would produce together that which would bring forth fruitfulness in abundance! They also were given authority at the same level. God told them that they would have dominion and that they would be able to subdue things under them. The words dominion and subdue in Genesis 1:28 gives us great insight about the level of authority released to them by God. The Hebrew word for dominion is the word "radah" and the Hebrew word for subdue in Hebrew is the word "kabash".

"Radah" means the power or right of governing and controlling; sovereign authority, refers to oversight of something that willingly submits. They are given the ability by God to watch over the works of His hands. They will rule over everything and it will willingly submit to them, they had complete dominion over the creation.

The word "kabash" means to conquer and bring into subjection or in others words making the things that don't want to submit, submit! He gave to them the ability to watch over the works of His hands, those things that would willingly submit but He also gave them the ability to put in line the things or thing that would not submit.

The account of the fall in Genesis Chapter 3 lets us know that there was an enemy of God lurking in the garden that was not going to willingly submit. What must be clear is that both the man and woman had the ability to handle the disobedient one. Many times we have discussed how Adam should have handled this problem, and he should have, but we must acknowledge that the woman had the ability to handle it as well. Because God gave **them** this authority, she didn't have to fall under the spell of the enemy or even have a conversation with him. She could have subdued him right at the beginning.

They had authority over everything living and moving on the earth and since this enemy had embodied something living and moving (the snake), she had full authority over it. We will investigate this later on, but it must be understood that she wasn't some weak creature who needed her husband to bail her out.

Genesis 2:7: and have dominion over the fish of the sea, and over the fowl of the air, and over every living thing that moveth upon the earth.

When she failed to operate in her authority then all of the responsibility fell on the man to handle the issue but as we know and will discuss later he didn't. For now it is important to realize the woman had the same level of authority and that they functioned as one.

Chapter 2: Worship

ೞ

"A woman is like a tea bag;
you never know how strong it
is until it's in hot water."

~Eleanor Roosevelt

ೞ

Genesis 1:26 And God said, Let us make man in our image,
let them have dominion over the fish of the sea, and over
the fowl of the air, and over the cattle, and over all the
earth, and over every creeping thing that creepeth upon
the earth. 27 So God created man in his own image, in the
image of God created he him; male and female created he
them. 28 And God blessed them, and God said unto them,
be fruitful, and multiply, and replenish the earth, and
subdue it.

Genesis 1:26-28 is known as the Dominion Mandate. The
man and woman are given dominion; they have rulership
because God gave it to them and all they did to gain it was
to be created in God's image. Discussing this chapter with
the majority of the church leaves no doubt that there is an
understanding about the dominion mandate. Mankind
(man and woman) is the supreme authority on earth and
everything is made for them. Without making light of the
dominion mandate, because this was carried out with

great responsibility is this all that the man and woman had to do in this place of paradise?

Genesis 2 gives further insight into why God created the man before the woman and what tasks he performed that no other creature could accomplish. Man's creation was very different from any other creature or thing created before him.

Genesis 2:7-8; *And the LORD God formed man of the <u>dust of the ground</u>, and breathed into his nostrils the breath of life; and man became a living soul. **8** And the LORD God planted a garden eastward in Eden; and there he put the man whom he had formed.*

Genesis 1 outlines the creation account detailing what occurred each day and that God spoke the things seen into existence. Once the Godhead makes the decision to create man, God actually comes down to earth and forms clay in an intimate fashion instead of just speaking. All of the accounts of creation before this point He spoke and it came forth. God said, "Let there be," and it was.

It Was Special

He comes down and with His hands fashions man from the clay which makes it intimate. I believe God follows this process because man had to be created in His image after His likeness.

Genesis 1:26 and 27 reveal that man and woman were created in the image of God is revealed but at this time neither of them are formed in the natural.

They were created and were communicated with spiritually before God comes down to form man in the natural. The additional step of molding the clay with His hands should speak volumes to us today about the importance God has placed on mankind. Next the couple is given authority over all of creation. An important principle is revealed here that must be understood: that *true authority should be received spiritually before it is handled in the natural.*
Through spiritual means God wants to be intimately involved with man in every aspect of his life.

Additional evidence of the importance of man to God is seen when He gives man breath. God takes the face of man in His hands and breathes the breath of God (Spirit) into his body and man awakens as a living soul. Have you thought about the fact that God kissed man so that life would come into his body? Through this intimate process man becomes a spiritual being that possesses a soul and lives in a body.

Breath enters the body and the soul was formed, which is the most precious possession anyone has. Man became a living soul. Living soul indicates that the soul is an independent life source. It gets direction from the spirit but it can live on its own without help from the spirit of man. Therefore the man has a spirit alive to God, a soul alive and a body alive giving him three living parts all making up one living being. Since man is in perfect unity with the LORD at this point and walking in spiritual authority the soul is functioning the way it was designed. This soul of man at this point is completely submitted to his spirit!

God communes with man's spirit which is the real existence of man and the spirit instructs the soul which directs the body. The soul which consists of his mind, his will and his emotions makes him unlike any other creature on the planet. But God places man in a controlled environment to learn obedience and to walk out his relationship.

The Proving Ground

Genesis 2:8 *And out of the ground made the LORD God to grow every tree that is pleasant to the sight, and good for food; the tree of life also in the midst of the garden, and the tree of knowledge of good and evil.*

It is an amazing thing that Adam has dominion over the whole earth, but God plants and puts him in the garden. He doesn't get to rule the whole earth even though he has total authority over everything. He's placed in the garden to prove out his authority and to develop his intimacy with God.

This principle operates the same way today, where God will give a person a little portion of the responsibility or authority promised before placing in their hands full responsibility or authority. God very seldom will give a person the greater first; He usually starts a person in the small and moves them into a place that amazes the person being used because it is so much greater than the starting place.

Job 8:7 Though thy beginning was small, yet thy latter end should greatly increase.

Ezekiel 36:11 And I will multiply upon you man and beast; and they shall increase and bring fruit: and I will settle you after your old estates, and will do better unto you than at your beginnings: and ye shall know that I am the LORD.

The Garden is a very large place watered with four water heads running through it from a river which flowed out of Eden. It is also important to understand that Eden wasn't the garden but the garden was in Eden. There is so much we have missed with this creation account of man and it hinders our understanding of the man and especially the woman. The bible tells us that it was the garden "of" Eden not that the garden was called Eden. When the bible tells us that the Garden of Eden was planted eastward in Eden, we should ask what was westward, northward and southward?

This garden had territory where gold and precious jewels were found covering the ground as decoration. Every kind of fruit bearing tree was there along with two very important trees, the tree of life and the tree of the knowledge of good and evil. Understanding the proving ground principle of the garden Adam was told not to eat of the tree of the knowledge of good and evil.

Genesis 2:10-12 And a river went out of Eden to water the garden; and from thence it was parted, and became into four heads. 11 The name of the first is Pison: that is it which compasseth the whole land of Havilah, where there is gold; 12 And the gold of that land is good: there is bdellium and the onyx stone.

Since everything is under the authority of man a conscience act of obedience or way to show his loyalty to God is not possible. God made man the Supreme Being on the earth and there was nothing greater.

Everything on the earth responded to him and followed his commands without question and for this reason one of the functions of the soul is almost completely uninvolved.

The commandment of God concerning the tree of the knowledge of good and evil was the only place where Adam had to exercise his will. Man had to decide to obey God in this one command so that he could fully function as a human being who used every part of his soul.

Every time he looked at the tree his soul was engaged and the decision (using his will) to obey God was planted deeper and deeper in his life. After this important point the bible gives insight into what work man was responsible for before his wife was created and presented to him.

Every man that is looking for a wife and every woman who would like to be married must understand the work that God gave man before the fall and that it should be functioning in his life before marriage.

Dress and Keep

*Genesis 2:15 And the LORD God took the man, and put him into the Garden of Eden to **dress it** and to **keep it**.*

When man is created everything else is already formed on the earth and operating the way God designed. Every plant and tree produces after its own kind. All of the animals are producing after their own kind and need no help from the man. Precious metals can be found all over the place which seem to be in the form of decorations. The beauty of the place is phenomenal. There is no need to produce a thing. God has already taken care of everything.

Man is placed in the garden to enjoy the animals, trees, the fruit and everything else provided by the hand of God. So there is nothing for Adam to do but enjoy the handiwork of God. So if there is nothing for him to plant then what is he doing? Maybe he had to rake the fallen leaves and groom the plants or things like that. The problem with that theory is the fact that nothing on the earth is dying because at this point there is no sin. The bible instructs that death comes where there is sin.

Romans 6:23 For the wages of sin is death; but the gift of God is eternal life through Jesus Christ our Lord.

We understand the concept of death and expect death because from the moment we were born we started dying. We have experienced death all around us in many different forms and it is found in some form in everything we can think of. We are accustomed to death, so much so that we declare that death is a part of life. That was not true for Adam. There was no death. There was only life.

If there's no death, then nothing is dying. If there's nothing dying then there are no rotten fruit, not a blade of grass withering, not a flower fading. Everything remains in its original and beautiful condition. If this is causing you problems in understanding then all you have to do is to think about heaven. There's no death in heaven. Hallelujah! You will die no more when you get to heaven. Isn't that awesome? Everything in heaven is forever increasing including the trees and plants.

In addition there's no more sickness, no more disease. Sickness and disease are things that were produced due to sin which causes death. Time also becomes a very important factor in life because we all have to die. When man was first created he was not subject to time. How do we know that? Because without sin there is no death so therefore there is no time to even mark.

It is my opinion that we wouldn't even keep up with birthdays because it wouldn't matter. The reason you keep up with birthdays is because you know you are going to die. Our lives are represented by the dash on the tombstone between the date of our birth and the date of our death. What would it matter how many birthdays we had if we knew death wasn't part of the equation?

Now since we realize man didn't have the duty of planting anything or the need to beautify and rake anything then what was he doing in the garden day by day? The bible clearly tells us what he was doing.

*Genesis 2:15 And the LORD God took the man, and put him into the Garden of Eden to **dress it** and to **keep it**.*

He was there to do two things and that was to dress and keep the garden.

The word *dress* in the verse is translated to work, till and even cultivate but we have already discussed and debunked these possibilities. The Hebrew word for Dress in the verse is "abad". This word does mean to work or labor which is the reason for it being translated work, till and cultivate in most bibles. But it is the extended definition that truly should be used to express the duty of the man in the garden, which is to worship from a priestly position.

That makes better sense because Adam was the only creature that could give God the willful worship that He deserved. This worship prepared the place for God to come down and fellowship with man on a daily basis. It is another way the soul of man becomes active in the garden experience.

Man was not there dealing with plants; he was there to give worth (worship) to the One who created all of greatness and beauty he was enjoying. The second word of importance is to keep, or better translated, protect, the place where he would worship.

Setting the Atmosphere

In most churches these days there are overhead projection units connected to computers with connection to the internet, but it would not be permissible for someone to project the Playboy Channel on the screen in church. That would be horrible, right? Okay, we won't go that far. Would it be alright to project most cable programs? Why not? Because the church is called the house of worship; it must stay free from everything that could cause distraction and be a place where there is no sin. It is dressed for God and His presence only.

The problem facing many church people is that they allow these shows in their homes that would not be allowed in their church building. Without speaking one word this declares that their homes are not a place of worship.

If our homes are not places of worship, then the enemy can come and dwell within them. When the enemy comes to dwell; people will try moving him out of their lives but the problem is they have unwittingly laid out a welcome mat and set the atmosphere for him. When he shows up most people will say he doesn't belong there. They will even rebuke him, but it is not proper to rebuke someone that has been invited.

Why would someone invite a person to their home and then rebuke him because he came? If we don't want a person in our homes, there shouldn't be an invitation extended. We must be people who understand how to dress (worship) the places where we dwell so that God can come and fellowship with us, and every place must be protected so that our fellowship with God is uninterrupted.

It was no different with Adam, who was responsible in the beginning to worship God and protect the garden from any and all things that could hinder his fellowship. We must do whatever is necessary to get in a place where we can worship God, and to cultivate an atmosphere that pleases God and invites His presence. At the same time we must resist any and every thing that would hinder our worship.

The garden was being dressed by a perfect man for the God of majesty to enjoy. All of the animals and plant life were taken to a higher level of experience through Adam's worship. As we will see this relationship will increase once the woman comes on the scene. It is the worship relationship that will keep everything in proper alignment with God.

Everything in the Garden was made perfect and remained that way until the time man disobeyed God and ate from the tree of the knowledge of good and evil. At that point everything that God proclaimed was good became contaminated with man's sin.

Herein is more proof that everything was created for man since the creations falls out of alignment with God's purpose after the disobedience of man.

The Bottom Line

In summary, the earth was perfect and God placed man and woman in the garden where they had fellowship with each other and especially with Him. But they didn't protect their position with Him and disobeyed the only commandment given and this caused them to fall from the place of perfection and fellowship with God. At that very moment everything changed. Christ came to bring man back to his first estate in God and restore the fellowship with God and each other. Therefore, those who have embraced the finished work of Jesus, the church, should be thinking and positioning themselves to live as pre-fall people who were without sin and not as fallen creatures still operating under the weight of sin and shame.

This is an easy statement to make but it can be difficult to live when everything around us is completely unlike anything Adam experienced before the fall. The greatness that Adam and his wife lived in is impossible to imagine when living outside of Christ and can be hard to enter into even once a person has given their life over to the Lord!

The best visual I can offer, which is still a very poor one, is for you to imagine being in a lush green valley with flowers so beautiful they look like they were painted onto the landscape. Listen to the sounds of the birds singing and the bees humming and the sound of deer rustling through the leaves. As you stand in this place and look out over the valley the cool breeze gently washes over you and everything seems right with the world and your life.
You return the next day to this same spot to enjoy the beautiful scene again and experience the same feeling you had the day before, but overnight there was a fire that burned the entire valley and all of the green is now gone and replaced with blackness and death. The sounds are gone and your nostrils are filled with the smell of smoke and ashes. There are no live animals in sight; many of them couldn't get out in time and their bodies are seen littered across the valley.

There would be a great sadness in your heart and instantly a desire to experience what was before will rise in your soul. The fall of Adam is much worse than this picture I paint! This entire creation is now struggling to be freed from the consequences of the fall. The bible declares that all of creation is groaning for the manifestation of the sons of God. The reason why people don't understand this is because they never saw the valley before it was burned so they think everything is normal.

Romans 8:19 -22 For the earnest expectation of the creature waited for the manifestation of the sons of God. [20] For the creature was made subject to vanity, not willingly, but by reason of him who hath subjected the same in hope, [21] Because the creature itself also shall be delivered from the bondage of corruption into the glorious liberty of the children of God. [22] For we know that the whole creation groaneth and travaileth in pain together until now.

In Genesis 1 and 2, a much different picture than the one Apostle Paul speaks of in Romans 8 is revealed. From the moment the Godhead determines that man would be created, it is understood that man would operate in the favor and ability of God. Nothing on the planet is groaning in any form of pain and everything is good!

Jesus came to restore the man, woman and every other thing affected by the fall. It is only through Jesus that we can see the valley before the fire.

Section 2: The Woman

Chapter 3: The Help Meet

*"A thing of beauty is a joy
for ever. Its loveliness
increases; it will never
Pass into nothingness; but
still will keep"*

~John Keats

And the LORD God said, it is not good that the man should
be alone; I will make him an help meet for him. Genesis
2:18

Take note what God didn't say, He didn't say that the man
was lonely.

As we saw in the previous chapter Adam is not lonely
because he is in fellowship with God. Loneliness can bring
feelings of depression and feelings of neediness, it can
force a person to focus on the need for companionship,
the need to be supported, and many other trappings that
come with loneliness.

But it is impossible to have the feelings of loneliness while
spending vital time with God. Adam walked with God daily

and was created for the good pleasure of God with the assignment of showing worth to God. This tells me that he had a full and very productive lifestyle. God give those who worship Him in spirit and truth a true sense of fulfillment.

One of the cautions I present to single adults is to not get married to attempt to overcome the feelings of loneliness. This is a recipe for failure! Because loneliness is a problem too deep and vast for another human being to fill, it can only be filled by the Lord!

God has a place in the human heart that can only be filled by Him and no one else! He left this hole in the heart so that man would desire Him and invite Him to fill it but many people attempt to fill it with work and careers or even other people just to find out that it is impossible to fill it with anything or anyone but God!

If you happen to be single and find yourself fighting feelings of loneliness, I'm sorry to say it this way, but you must check your relationship with the Lord. It is my personal experience that God will fill every lonely place in your life. You can't be lonely when you spend time with God. It is impossible! He won't let it happen!

Alone With God

Moses spent forty days and forty nights on the mountain with God and was never lonely. He was alone, but he was never lonely. The bible indicates that God had to make him return to the people in the valley and leave the mountain where the presence of God dwelt.

Think about spending eternity in the presence of God and never getting enough of His presence and glory. With this in mind, how can we have a vital relationship with God on earth and have loneliness invade our lives? When your relationship with God is where it should be, a human companion could feel as though they are getting in the way of your relationship with God.

During times where worship is expressed, words of love and joy are conveyed, fulfilling many of our emotional needs. Then there are statements such as; why would I leave You? Lord, You are my sufficiency. You are everything to me. Father, You are my all in all. Lord, You make me feel greater than I can feel with any person. You fulfill every crack and crevice of my life. Amen!

It is very important that you find this vital place before entering into a relationship with anyone; I call it the "God and you" relationship. Your entire life will be energized and the joy of the Lord will be your strength! I know it can sound old fashioned and even a little odd, but He can still take care of you.

There are many things we say in our church experience that has not become a reality in our lives: He can be a mother to the motherless. He can be a father to the fatherless. He can be a friend to the friendless. These are things we say just to make our souls feel better about what we are experiencing.

We also use these statements to console someone else who is facing life's problems, but the sayings haven't become reality to us until our "God relationship" is firm. What am I saying? If you are lonely, you've got to find time to be alone with God!

Not a church relationship; a vital personal, God and you, relationship. I'm talking about a time when you talk to the Lord like you talk to every other friend you know. Stop thinking in religious terms, just talk with God without trying to form your sentences in King James Bible language. Just be yourself and learn to enjoy the relationship that God desires to have with you.

God's Timing

Adam is engaged in a vital relationship with God and God makes the decision that it isn't good that man should worship alone. Notice that Adam didn't ask God for a wife, it was a Godhead decision. God determined that the timing was right for the woman to be created so that the man and woman could begin to function in their oneness.

So God makes him a help *meet*. The word "meet" in this passage shouldn't be translated "mate" because it will completely change the purpose of the creation of the woman and in many ways devalue her even before she is presented to the man. The word mate indicates that

Adam had a need to mate and that God created the woman for his needs to be fulfilled. To be fruitful, multiply and replenish the earth was absolutely a part of the dominion mandate but this was so that the earth would be filled with humans who would have a relationship with God! We clearly understand that the woman is vital to this mandate becoming a reality but it must be understood that the first couple wasn't motivated by their flesh or any other natural desire.

God created her to first help "meet" the responsibility that Adam had to dress and keep the garden. God did not determine that it was time for Adam to no longer be alone because He wanted him to "mate," which would have only met the need of Adam. But she was created so that they could in full agreement worship their Creator.

Remember, in Genesis 1, God was speaking to them and gave them dominion over all creation. Therefore, the woman was just as capable as the man to exercise the authority set forth by God. She also had a relationship with God that completely fulfilled the creative purposes designed for "Them!"

In Genesis 2, the order of human creation is discussed and has more to do with communion than it has to do with supremacy. Adam learned the importance of worshiping God alone, before he had the responsibility of loving and communing with his wife. The woman was created to join the man in his communion so that she could worship with him. This should be the model women follow today; a woman should join a worshipping man in his pursuit of God. She can recognize this man because of her own commitment to worship and the importance placed on the relationship she has with God.

God used an interesting word to identify the woman who would join the man in worship. He called her a "helpmeet!" Many of our bibles translated this word to mean "helpmate," but from my studies this is an improper transliteration. This was done because of the way we view things after the fall (sin) of mankind. As I mentioned earlier it is my belief that God had a much greater and extensive plan for the woman then just to be the mate for the man.

The Hebrew word for "meet" in Genesis 2:18 is the word "neged," pronounced "neh- ghed." This word can be found in the Strong's Concordance with the reference number 5048 and it means:

1. what is in front of (adv)
2. in front of, straight forward, before, in sight of
3. in front of oneself, straightforward
4. before your face, in your view or purpose with (prep)
5. what is in front of, corresponding to
6. in front of, before
7. in the sight or presence of
8. parallel to
9. over, for
10. in front, opposite
11. at a distance (prep)
12. from the front of, away from
13. from before the eyes of, opposite to, at a distance from
14. from before, in front of
15. as far as the front of

Notice that the word for "meet (neged), has absolutely nothing to do with mating. The word carries the understanding about what the position of the woman is in relationship to the man.

She is to be in front, before, in the sight of, in front of one's self, straight forward, before your face, in your view or purpose. That doesn't fit the societal view of a woman's position because society says that she belongs behind the man. "Behind every good man there is a good woman." It is not the way God designed her and it doesn't fulfill her purpose. The above quote is spoken from pulpits, platforms, television, dinner tables and in counseling sessions, but this is a lie from hell and most women have embraced it and now quote it as truth.

God did not make the woman to help the man become more important or successful, since both of them were already made in the image of God and had all of the ability needed to completely fulfill the duties and authority set forth by God.

After man's disobedience in the Garden where they ate from the tree of the knowledge of good and evil, the woman was placed in a servant role. From that point on, women were looked upon as instruments to fulfill man's needs and desires. In the truest sense, they were devalued!

It is for this reason that a woman should embrace and accept the finished work of Christ, because it is through

Christ that she is restored to her designed position. She is brought back to her valued place and first estate, which was in the beginning as one with the man in every way. Christianity is the only religion that provides for women to be restored to this place. None of the other religions provide this place for women; they are still placed in subservient roles to men.

In many cases they are disregarded completely, sold as slaves, treated harshly, raped and even killed without any true remorse. This is because they are not much better than an animal in the eyes of the men of those religious societies and sects. There are even church organizations that still will not allow women the freedom to be used at their designed level. In no way would they have given the first message delivered after the resurrection of Christ to a woman. But Jesus did!

Reviewing the position that society declares a woman should take in relation to a man shows us how much she has been devalued.

"Behind every good man is a good woman!" This is one of the most famous of quotes that speaks of the position of women. Therefore, this quote must be one of the first sayings to be destroyed out of the church and societal mindset.

One of the things we know is that the man is called to be the protector of his family and loved ones. Consider that there is a spiritual enemy who is doing everything in his power to destroy life and vision. If the woman is behind the man in an effort to somehow help him accomplish his life goals, then he cannot protect her back from the attack of this enemy.

She can be attacked from the back side and the man really can't do anything about it if she is back there pushing him. It is my belief that this is one of the reasons so many woman struggle with self-worth and lack purpose in their lives. They think it is their position in life to make the man great!

It has also been strongly suggested that the woman should be on the man's side in a place equal with him. Returning to the first example concerning the spiritual enemy and the man being the protector, the man is now in a better position to see the woman he is instructed to protect, but she is still exposed. This tells me the enemy still has an entry point into the life of this woman. I submit to you that behind or beside the man is not the proper position for the woman in a man's life.

Remember, the definition for "helpmeet" has to do with being positioned out in front. This is where she belongs. Why does she belong in front of the man? First, it is a place of complete safety and there is nothing that can attack or harm her without him seeing it; her back is no longer exposed as it is in the other two positions mentioned previously. The focus of the man must first be on her and not on his work or life goals; he must understand that she isn't positioned to make him great. He is positioned to protect and provide for *her*. For them together to focus their undivided attention on the God who created everything and to worship Him for the greatness and goodness they enjoy through His love. Worship is so important because it is from this place that God gives prayer instruction and vision is received that the couple will have responsibility over.

When the woman is properly positioned, she has the duty of announcing the vision and purpose of the union and how the two of "them" will accomplish it. Even though she is positioned in front, it doesn't place her in headship. Some men have difficulty with this principle because they've been taught that headship means being in front and leading. A general can lead from the back of the pack. He is not diminished in rank because he is giving orders away from the frontlines.

A Natural Example

The majority of people in the United States of America have absolutely no idea who Wilson Livingood is or what he did for a living. Mr. Livingood was the Sergeant- at Arms of the United States House of Representatives for 17 years, and he functioned as the chief law enforcement officer of the House. Mr. Livingood has recently retired and Mr. Paul D. Irving now holds the position.

The Sergeant-at- Arms is responsible for security in the House wing of the United States Capitol, the House office buildings, and on adjacent grounds. It was Mr. Livingood performing one of his many duties that helped confirm the importance of a woman's position in front of her husband announcing their purpose to the society.

During the State of the Union address Mr. Livingood stood in the doorway of the Congress and addressed the speaker of the House, saying, "Mr. Speaker, the President of the United States of America." He announced and then proceeded to usher the president down the hall to the platform. He was responsible for the announcement and for walking out in front, but it didn't make him the president.

The difference with the woman's announcement is that she is announcing her husband and by doing so she is also announcing herself.

The Spiritual Example

*1Corinthians 15:45-47 And so it is written, The **first man Adam** was made a living soul; the **last Adam** was made a quickening spirit. [46] Howbeit that was not first which is spiritual, but that which is natural; and afterward that which is spiritual. [47] The first man is of the earth, earthy: the second man is the Lord from heaven.*

Jesus is the last Adam and it must be understood that He is not the second Adam. If He came as the second Adam then there could be a third, but He is the last and final Adam. To completely restore what the first Adam lost Jesus must have a woman (wife) to join with Him. Those

55

who attend church services regularly undoubtedly have heard speakers refer to the church as the bride of Christ. The main point through this reference is that the church is one with Christ in every way as His body. We will examine this point further later in this book, but for now suffice it to say that the same position the man and the woman were in from the beginning Jesus and the church complete now!

Ephesians 5:25 Husbands, love your wives, even as Christ also loved the church, and gave himself for it...

Think about the position of the church on the earth today it is as a woman announcing her husband who is Jesus Christ to any and all who will listen.

She's (the church) announcing that He's coming, she's announcing His greatness, and she's announcing the purpose of the One that she's in unity with ("Therefore if any man be in Christ..."). Most men and women identify with this fact that the church is one with Christ having the responsibilities listed. But these same people have somehow completely overlooked that the union between a man and woman is designed to model the spiritual union between Christ and His church.

The Proper Position

When couples understand that the woman was created to meet the responsibility given, then they will stand together before God in their right positions in full surrender and worship. In Genesis 2:15 God told Adam to "dress and keep" the Garden, which we have recognized as worship and worship protection. After his relationship is established with God, God makes the decision to create the woman to join in this responsibility.

Therefore, the greatest thing that couple can do together is to worship God. They are not called to pray first. Believe me, I have nothing against prayer; you can read my books, "Numbered with the Transgressors," or "The Power is in the Closet," on the subject of prayer and see my passion on this subject. But it is from the place of worship where the prayer focus that God wants will be realized.

Notice in the following passages when the disciples asked Jesus to teach them to pray, He instructed His disciples to first enter into worship before offering petitions to God.

Luke 11:2 And he said unto them, When ye pray, say, Our Father which art in heaven, Hallowed be thy name. Thy kingdom come. Thy will be done, as in heaven, so in earth.

Our Father which art in Heaven, hallowed be Thy name – first worship, we hallow Your name before we ask for anything. Before we consider provision, our job first is to worship God. Hallowed be Thy name!

Once a person or couple understands how to truly worship and hallow the name of the Lord, advancing beyond this place can be a challenge. Giving worth to God and His greatness fulfills our deepest emotional desires. It is not an easy transition to move from this place. God dwells in our worship and that makes moving away from it difficult.

It is Jesus who tells the Samarthian woman that "God is seeking worshippers."

John 4:21-24 Jesus saith unto her, Woman, believe me, the hour cometh, when ye shall neither in this mountain, nor yet at Jerusalem, worship the Father. [22] Ye worship ye know not what: we know what we worship: for salvation is of the Jews. [23] But the hour cometh, and now is, when the true worshippers shall worship the Father in spirit and in truth: for the Father seeketh such to worship him. [24] God is a Spirit: and they that worship him must worship him in spirit and in truth.

It is understood that the Lord wants His followers to be led by the Spirit and full of truth but He is primarily looking for worshippers. Jesus didn't tell the woman that God was looking for people praying; though we know the importance Jesus places on prayer. "My house will be called a house of prayer for all people" is one of His teachings, but the foundation of the house is worship (Luke 19:46).

The proper positioning for the man and woman in a relationship is first to stand before God and declare His worth and greatness. When a woman carries this attitude into her relationship with the man in her life, he will be empowered by God to accomplish for her what she can never accomplish through other means. When a woman positions herself to speak well of her husband or the men in her life and the man understands that it is sincere, he will willingly protect, support, and provide anything that she needs. It becomes one of his greatest joys to make her happy!

The problem is many women today have positioned themselves in front of their man and have turned to face him instead of facing forward to announce their unified purpose.

When a woman turns and faces the man, he is then duty bound to defend his position, which instantly causes confrontation. Even though the woman is one with her husband, when she turns and faces him she becomes his competition instead of his completion. Remember, the man is designed to protect his family against foreign and domestic enemies. But when she turns to the front and announces their purpose and vision, he can't fight, so he turns his attention to support and love. Women can get most men to love and adore them just by getting in their proper position.

The majority of men on the earth want a woman to know who she is and how to function in her position, because it allows him to be a man to her and give his life and attention to her. This doesn't even have to be a romantic situation; it could just be a regular friendship or working relationship.

The first woman as a help meet was designed to operate in the same authority and abilities as her husband Adam without any distinction whatsoever. The worship of God by Adam and Mrs. Adam was the very thing that further separated them from the animals. Their love and honor for each other was only second to the love and honor they had for the Godhead.

Couples who find this place will find a well of blessings that will advance them into new and exciting places with God *and* man.

Chapter 4: The End of Creation

❦

"A beautiful woman uses her lips for Truth, her voice for Kindness, her ears for Compassion, her hands for Charity and her heart for Love. For those who do not like her, she uses Prayer"

~Jolly Rutten

❦

Adam is no longer alone in the Garden because God made the decision to create the woman as his help meet. The creation of man was intimate and was no different with the woman. God came down and fashioned her with His hands and breathed life into her body, except this time there was a slight twist to the creation process which helps to demonstrate how God saw and valued the woman. This value she regains in Christ, once she embraces His finished work on the cross.

The bible explains how each creature was formed and how each of them received their names so that there would be a clear contrast between the animals and humans.

Genesis 2:19 And out of the ground the LORD God formed every beast of the field, and every fowl of the air; and brought them unto Adam to see what he would call them: and whatsoever Adam called every living creature, that was the name thereof.

The above passage is very interesting from the point of view that Adam gave names to all of the animals, not God. Genesis 1 indicates that God named everything else, so why didn't He stay with that process and name the animals also?

Naming rights allowed Adam to operate in the dominion mandate God gave to them in the beginning. It would have been too easy for God to name each animal and introduce Adam to them, but He didn't. God gave Adam that responsibility and agreed with his decision.

The bible declares that Adam gave names to all cattle, now that seems redundant doesn't it? But it isn't! He actually gave names to each animal, which is what still happens on farms all over the world. We still name our animals, bringing them closer to us and eliminating the need to just call the dog, "dog," or the cat, "cat." Names are very important, since they give the person, place or thing its identity and purpose.

Therefore, in order to name anything you must understand it. We name businesses, buildings, ministries, churches, foods, planets, galaxies and anything that needs to be identified. In order for a man to name a new medication, he has to first understand what the medication is meant to do.

The chemist can't bring the new medication to someone like me and ask me to name it so that the public can understand its value and purpose. I can't determine what to call the medication because I don't know what it consists of, or the result it is designed to produce.

I can't confidently name what I don't understand. By God allowing Adam the right to name the animals, Adam had to understand their purpose and design. This also sealed the fact that man was the authority over the earth and everything found on it. The next thing that we are told could sound a bit strange if we didn't have an understanding about what it meant to dress the garden. God told Adam to look for a help meet among the animals that he had named and now rules over.

Genesis 2:20 And Adam gave names to all cattle, and to the fowl of the air, and to every beast of the field; but for Adam there was not found an **help meet** *for him.*

God told Adam to go amongst the animals to search for a help meet so that he would be perfectly sure that there was nothing already created that could help dress the garden (worship).

Adam wasn't attempting to find a mate among the animals, but he was looking for a help meet.
God would have never violated creation to have Adam look amongst the animals for something to mate with. God wanted Adam to find that one animal that was on his level and could function as a priest before Him, to worship Him and have the ability to protect the place of worship that He gave him. Adam came back to God convinced that there was nothing already created that could accomplish this task with him.

Since there was nothing already created, it was clear that God would have to create it. Adam was instructed to find among the animals something that could and would do what he was able to do, so the person God would create had to have all of his abilities.

And the LORD God caused a deep sleep to fall upon Adam, and he slept: and he took one of his ribs, and closed up the flesh instead thereof; Genesis 2:21

The Hebrew word used for rib is *Tsela`* which means side, rib or beam. Even though God takes the man's rib, it can be easily viewed as his entire side.

And the rib, which the LORD God had taken from man, made he a woman, and brought her unto the man. Genesis 2:22

We are not told how long Adam slept; it is my belief that he slept three days. The reason I hold to this idea is in conjunction with Jesus' death, burial and resurrection.

For three days Jesus slept, and when He was resurrected from His sleep, His bride was also birthed. While Jesus walked the earth, He was completely responsible for the worship and the protection of the worship, but He spoke about the church that would be birthed (His bride) that would operate in the same authority that He had.

Matthew 16:18, 19 And I say also unto thee, That thou art Peter, and upon this rock I will build my church; and the gates of hell shall not prevail against it. [19] And I will give unto thee the keys of the kingdom of heaven: and whatsoever thou shalt bind on earth shall be bound in heaven: and whatsoever thou shalt loose on earth shall be loosed in heaven.

John_14:12 Verily, verily, I say unto you, He that believeth on me, the works that I do shall he do also; and greater works than these shall he do; because I go unto my Father.

Jesus went as far as saying that the church would be equal in ability as He was while walking on the earth. As we have already seen, Jesus is referred to as the last Adam, and His church as a bride.

Genesis 2:23 And Adam said, This is now bone of my bones, and flesh of my flesh: she shall be called Woman, because she was taken out of Man.

God brought the woman to Adam and again, He doesn't name her because that was Adam's responsibility. Just like with the animals that Adam named, in order for Adam to name the woman, he had to know and understand her purpose.

He could not name her without knowing her purpose and understanding how she would function in that purpose. I have heard men many times proclaim that they don't understand women, but when you really think about it that can't be true.

I tell men this all over the nation: you do understand her, because you named her. The issue is not one of understanding, but rather one of ignoring or refusing to study her. If a man ignores the woman in his life, it will appear that he doesn't understand her because he hasn't taken time to study her.

A man should study the woman to know what she likes and why she likes it. It is not enough to react to her face frowning, but to know why she frowns. Many times men have not placed the proper value on the woman and have her as an appendix in his life instead of the crown of his life.

When a woman doesn't know who she is in God or the value she brings to the man, she will allow herself to be devalued in this way and many others. Then there are women who will take the defensive attitude, announcing that no man will take advantage of her, or proclaiming she doesn't need a man to do what is in her heart.

These are true statements, but it is not what God designed for her. The woman never has to become defensive or stubborn to move a man's heart in the direction that she wants. When I make this statement, I am referring to a man who is without issues in his own life and understands who he is as the source of strength and love for the woman in his life. The man, who has decided to use women for his purposes or is abusive to women, may never respond, no matter what the woman does.

This is the reason why a woman shouldn't first seek to be the mate to the man but rather a help meet with the man. Find out if this man has a vision for life, spends time before God in worship, prayer and studying the word, and if his vision is one that you want to be a part of.

Ask him what was the last thing he failed at and why? Listen very carefully to the answer, because it tells you if he will succeed later in life and if you can join his team as a help meet. Listen to find out if he places the blame on others, or if he takes most of the blame and has a plan to never experience that type of failure again.

Did he depend on God for the answer and did he receive godly counsel about the failure? Remember, everyone on this earth has and will fail but it is how you deal with the failures that will help you to advance in life. It is not what you go through that determines your worth, but how you go through it that makes all of the difference in the world. The way he values his work, or life itself, will give you great insight into how he will value you and your opinions in his life. Will this man allow you to be properly positioned to help meet the vision responsibilities of his life while helping you to increase in the assignments God has given you?

Many women have decided to attract men to their bodies instead of attracting them to their ability to complete him. Therefore they have misrepresented themselves as only a piece of meat, instead of a valuable asset to help advance the man in his God given role through focused and intentional worship. Mrs. Adam came from the side of Adam and when she was brought back to him, she became his completeness.

When a woman is being pursued by a man, she must ask if he is the one she should be joined to in completeness and not just in sex. The generation has fallen so far largely due to the fact women have forgotten their value and have made it extremely easy for men to accomplish their goal of sexual pleasure without having to provide anything in return.

A woman was not designed to first provide man with sexual pleasure. She was designed to help him in his pursuit toward God and to make the heart of God happy. Since the fall, women have been devalued to just a piece of meat, when the entire issue of sex is more about her fulfillment than his.

We will discuss this in the next chapter, but in a nutshell sexual intimacy was designed more for the woman than the man!

Section 3: The Sound

Chapter 5: The Womb

The sentence at the end of Chapter 4 has caused men in men's meetings to almost faint. They will yell out, "Bishop, you need to explain that statement!" Everyone gets a good laugh out of the request for clarity about who should be the beneficiary of the sexual experience.

Now it is without question that men enjoy sex, and should, since God created it. But most men have not taken time to view things before the disobedience and the fall that followed.

Remember, it is the man that named the woman and it is this very name that puts most of this in perspective. Adam said, "She is bone of my bones and flesh of my flesh; she shall be called "Woman".

If we separate this word "Woman" into two parts, it gives us "Wo" and "Man;" if the first part of the word is identifying her distinction from the man, it would represent her womb. Therefore it could be said that she is a man with a womb.

Yes, this is a sexual organ but it is my belief that God had a higher purpose, which was to bring forth living creatures into the earth to replenish it. Sure, this means having sex and sex is without a doubt pleasurable, but God's design goes beyond human pleasure.

God partnered with the woman to bring humans into the earth so that it would be replenished. God could have come down and created each person, but then they would all be connected to God and not each other. By allowing the human race to come through the birth canal, a two way connection was established between God who created the first man and woman, and the parents of the new born.

At the time woman is created and presented to Adam, there is no evidence that they would disobey God. But we know now that they did and all of creation was flung into major disarray. Man and woman found themselves outside of the covenant relationship they had enjoyed to that point.

God instantly put a plan into action designed to restore the relationship He had with the first family. This plan had to do with Jesus coming to earth as a man. Since the earth was given to man, Jesus couldn't come as God or as an angel to fix the problem. Since a man caused the problem it would take a man to fix the problem.

The Gateway

Jesus (Immanuel, God with us) needed a way to enter the earth and the only way to come was through a woman's womb. Therefore, we can say that God created the womb as His legal entrance into the earth.

Genesis 3:14 And the LORD God said unto the serpent, Because thou hast done this, thou art cursed above all cattle, and above every beast of the field; upon thy belly shalt thou go, and dust shalt thou eat all the days of thy life:

Genesis 3:15 And I will put enmity between thee and the woman, and between thy seed and her seed; it shall bruise thy head, and thou shalt bruise his heel.

These passages of scripture are associated with the punishment handed down by God after the disobedience in the garden by the Adams. This is the punishment directed towards the enemy Satan who embodied the serpent and beguiled the woman. The punishment has to do with her seed identified as a male crushing the head of the enemy and the enemy only being able to bruise his heel.

Nothing is spoken of Adam's (man's) seed being involved in this process. Since Jesus would be born of a virgin and not by the natural use of a man this again reveals the partnership God had with the woman so that His Son would have a way into the earth to redeem mankind. The issues we face to today, especially those concerning the womb, have as much to do with the hatred Satan has for all mankind but particularly the woman who was the vessel used as a portal from heaven to earth for Jesus who defeated and destroyed the works of hell.

Jesus is the Son of God and is referred to as the last Adam but he wasn't created like the first Adam. He came through the birth canal and had to depend on a woman (Mary) to carry Him to term. In this way Jesus completely identified with man from conception to death.

When the miracle of childbearing and what actually takes place in the womb over the course of a pregnancy is examined, it is absolutely mind blowing. As a man, I have lamented to God and before people that it is not fair that a woman can experience this awesome miracle and I can't.

Men who hear this statement thank God that they cannot give birth and women indicate that they wish I could. It's not that I long to go through the pain of childbirth. For me it has to do with the amazing miracle of life that is developing inside the body of another human.

Many women haven't really appreciated the fact that a person is growing inside of her womb. Eyes, ears, a nose, a mouth, legs and arms, a brain and much more are forming; coming from a tiny seed. This is the miracle of birth and only women can experience it.

In this hour, the womb is not a safe place. It is clear that the enemy has attacked the woman and the partnership agreement between her and God to bring new life into the earth. We have allowed the destruction of 55 million unborn babies in the United States over the last forty years, since the decision by the Supreme Court on abortion rights, Roe v. Wade. The 40th anniversary of this decision will be observed on January 22, 2013.

The enemy hates the womb because it was through the womb that Jesus came and it is through Jesus that death, hell and the grave are defeated.

There are many women sitting in churches all over America carrying and hiding the shame of having had one or more abortions with no one to tell. God doesn't want you to be bound by this secret any longer; all you need to do is to ask Him to forgive you and re-enter your partnership with Him.

Even if you are past child bearing age it is your duty to instruct younger women about the importance of and the relationship God has with the woman and her womb.

There is an entire movement that rejects the natural use of the womb (gay men) and denies access to the natural use of the womb (lesbian women). The homosexual agenda has framed their argument around civil rights when it is really an issue of the womb.

Many women support the homosexual agenda and the idea of people having the right to love anyone they choose but the issue is much deeper than that, it is the fact Satan truly hates women and her designed purpose of carrying life in partnership with God!

The entire pornography industry is an attack against the womb. Through pornography the womb is perverted and appears to be designed for the desired use of the men engaged in the sex act and the ones viewing the act through whatever medium is used. Either way it is an issue of the womb and the sad thing is most woman I talk to aren't aware of these things.

Back to the Sex Talk

Remember it is my position that sex is primarily designed for women. I base this entirely on the design of the woman's womb and how she enters into the sexual encounter. Most women connect sex to their hearts, whereas men connect sex to their minds. All that is needed for a man is the thought, but it takes much more for most women to be prepared for intimacy. We will discuss this fact even more in the following chapter.

The other tell-tale sign is that most men will experience the release they desire when entering the physical relationship. But this doesn't hold true for the woman.

When she experiences a release, it is far more intense and more frequent than the man's; she can also experience four different types of orgasms. There are women who attend my meetings who didn't know this and ask men (me) to explain what it is they should be experiencing. When women are asked about their sexual release many of them report that they have never had or seldom have any type of release. This causes everyone to have a great laugh but the person who asked wasn't joking she really wanted to know. Well, they are vaginal, clitoral, G- spot and full body orgasms. When these four types of orgasms are presented, questions arise for those who have not experienced them.

A woman can experience all of the releases multiple times during the sexual experience. Each release point is far more intense than what a man experiences. Herein is one of main reasons I tell men that sex isn't primarily for them because if a man had any of these, no doubt it would kill him instantly.

Hidden and Precious

Another reason sex is primarily for women is due to the actual makeup of the womb. Unless there is some type of birth defect a woman is born with a hymen and it is just sitting there with no apparent purpose.

The hymen is of great importance because it is designed to seal the marriage covenant. In every covenant there are two parts, the oath and the blood seal.

When a man and woman are married, they stand before an officiant with witnesses to declare their love, which is the oath. But the wedding isn't official until they consummate the marriage. God gave a woman the hymen placed safely inside of her womb to be broken during intercourse and to seal the covenant agreement.

God didn't give this to the man, but to the woman with the responsibility to safeguard it until her day of matrimony. Until the blood seal is applied, the covenant is not sealed and therefore not in full effect.
For the Christian, there is a promise in 2 Corinthians that removes the guilt if a woman has released this seal to someone other than her husband.

In the days of my sin life I learned that if a virgin woman would give herself to me and her hymen was broken she would do almost anything for me. Her parents or friends couldn't get her to leave me because the seal designed for her husband had been given away. In my meeting we have broken the power of this hold on women's lives so they can live free. If you have released your seal to someone other than your spouse then it is time for you to get free.

2 Corinthians 5:17 Therefore if any man be in Christ, he is a new creature: old things are passed away; behold, all things are become new.

80

Receive the fact that old things are gone and you are forgiven.

Thank God for His forgiveness, but it is not the way things were designed. Since the disobedience in the Garden, men have used the woman and discounted what God placed in her. It is time that women began to live in the valued way God designed. It is also time for women to help their sisters understand who they are and what they are carrying.

Not Talked About at Church

When I speak to men about this subject, they are still holding on to the hope that sex could be designed around their needs and conquests. But once the subject of the clitoris is brought up in church, you can normally hear a pin hit the floor.

The clitoris is a part of the womb that has absolutely no other function then pleasure. God gave it to the woman who can have multiple orgasmic experiences of several types. Everything that the man has in his genitalia has dual purposes. Men have constantly heard about sowing their wild oats and conquests; but it all depends on using a woman as a devalued piece of meat.

Women have bought into this mindset and provided their bodies, advertised their bodies and sold their bodies all for the pleasure of men. The devil in hell is rolling on the ground laughing, because the very thing that God used to enter the earth and that will seal the marriage covenant is being used to destroy lives, marriages and even take life through the abortion process.

When your mother told you to cross your legs and to say no, she knew what she was talking about, even though she might not have said it the way I have in this book. It is now time for women everywhere to teach other women, and especially young women, their value. Mature women must teach younger women to stop thinking of themselves as a plaything for men and realize they are a valued God given blessing.

All over America young women have determined that they have little or no value and will perform all types of sexual acts in an attempt to satisfy young men. These young men have no clue about how God has valued the woman and don't want to know since their needs are being fulfilled.

In section six I will discuss the movement that is needed which involves having a mature woman train a younger woman in the ways and purposes of God. This is of great importance so that we don't lose an entire generation of women to a devious society. As a woman if you agree that a true movement is needed to restore value to today's women, I am asking you to get started today!

Chapter 6: Cleaving

*Don't be in a relationship
where you have to question the
other person's love for you.*

ഇ)ca

*Genesis 2:24-25 Therefore shall a man leave his father and
his mother, and shall cleave unto his wife: and they shall
be one flesh. And they were both naked, the man and his
wife, and were not ashamed.*

Genesis 2:24 is an amazing passage of scripture, in that it
gives the blueprint for joining a man and woman together
in marriage. Notice that the man is instructed to leave his
mother and father. A question could be asked why is the
man instructed to leave his parents with no mention of the
woman leaving her parents. First, it is clearly understood
that the woman is joining the man in the same way Mrs.
Adam was brought to Adam. Secondly, he must change his
focus and desires of pleasing his parents to now pleasing
his wife by cleaving to her.

The majority of men in North America have very little
understanding about cleaving because the society has

taught him that it is a sign of weakness. He will do everything and anything in his power to make other men think that he is the man who has the woman cleaving to him instead of him cleaving to her. When women seek men or become easy prey for men, then there's no need for him to ever embrace the understanding of cleaving.

The definition of cleaving is to cling, stick, stay close, keep close, keep to, follow closely, join to, over take, catch, to cling, stay with, be joined together, cause to cleave, to pursue closely, and overtake to be made to cling.

God designed relationships in such a way that the woman would never forget how much He values her by the constant pursuit of the man. It is not the job of the woman to follow closely, chase, or overtake the man.

Many women have changed the creative order by chasing men; by doing so they have messed things up. The creative order was that women were to be chased after, pursued, and shown worth. I will expand on this fact later in the chapter, but it wasn't Mrs. Adam's assignment to provide for Adam, it was her assignment to join him in the garden to accomplish his God given purpose.

In this hour, many women have worked hard and possess much more than the men she is in contact with, largely because men aren't taught to prepare themselves to provide for the woman he will cleave to.

The younger women of this generation are so confused it's amazing. It appears that they think it is their duty to take care of the men in their lives. Then they will complain when these same men take advantage of them, or cheat with other women while being with them. Everything about the relationship with the man told him that it was all about him, so why complain about your own creation?

A woman has to know her worth. And if you diminish yourself, the man will absolutely diminish you. Women must change their attitudes about pursuing men without becoming negative against men, which will make the best man run away as fast as possible.

In some cases, women will punish men for trying to cleave by thinking of them as soft or less than a man because he asked her out again too soon. It is clear when the man is very interested in a woman or if he is stalking her with wrong intentions and motives. But when it is a pursuit from a well balanced man it is his duty to cleave. God has made him that way, so it is not fair to penalize him for doing what he is designed to do.

Could this be another reason Adam was created first and left alone in the garden to develop a desire for the woman that only God in His timing would bring forth? It is clear that once Adam was created, he had a need and the need he had was the woman. But when God created the woman, she didn't have a need at all.

Adam had to wait for God to decide the woman should come forth. When she was created she was the end of human creation and everything she could ever need was already provided for her.

Think about this momentous day when Adam awakes to this awesomely beautiful woman who is made in the likeness and image of God just like he was. She was someone who could actually join him in his assigned duty of dressing and protecting the Garden of Eden. God had prepared him in every way for her coming by providing him with the abundance of the garden and a relationship with the Godhead.

The woman is not the source of provisions or income, nor is she the one who has to introduce the man to God. This is one of the main reasons why the modern day pattern of women taking care of men is so out of order. There are women who seek the Lord and then settle for the man who doesn't know or even acknowledge the God that she is serving.

Once a woman uses her possessions to help win a man she tremendously devalues herself and in many cases can never regain the place of value that she so rightly deserves.

It is and has always been the role of the man to pursue the woman and provide for her in every way. Give him the easy way out and I guarantee he will take it!

The man is supposed to be the giver; the woman should be the receiver. Your anatomy declares the fact that man is the giver and the woman is the receiver. Therefore, the position of the man is not only to give in intimacy, but to give in everything. The bible declares that a man is to give his life for his wife.

Ephesians 5:25 Husbands love your wives even as Christ loved the church and gave himself for it.

So Christ gave, and the man is in the same position. He has to give and the woman must take the position of the church, living in a continual position to receive.

When a woman moves from the receiving position, she upsets the way the man is to cleave to her and pursue her. Yes, he must pursue you with all that's in him and you must allow him to do so, without making it too easy.

This is not a game! God didn't design this so that a woman could use it as a carrot out in front of the horse that he can never obtain. Once a man senses a woman is playing with his emotions, he will quickly move on to the next assignment.

Also notice that the instruction given by Adam is that a man leaves his father and mother to cleave to his wife. He didn't have girlfriends in mind, only wives. But now many men have forgotten how to cleave to their wives in the way they attempted to show during the dating process.

When the husband is still pursuing the wife it tells her just how much he loves and values her; that she hasn't become his live-in servant who does all of the things he doesn't want to and is there to fulfill his sexual fantasies. Rather, she has become one with him in every way so when he makes her happy he is actually making himself happy.

Ephesians 5:28 So ought men to love their wives as their own bodies. He that loveth his wife loveth himself.

Cleaving to the woman is the man's responsibility and allowing him to cleave is the woman's. It is sad that I have to instruct Christian women to flirt with their husbands, but this will help him to remember and desire to cleave. Men have a hunter mentally, which is to track, wait and bag the game so that the head can be mounted on the wall. Once on the wall there is no need to do any of the things he did to catch the animal. Now all he does is to talk about how he caught the animal and relives that process over and over.

Since he romanticizes the pursuit, the desire to pursue is strong and he needs to have the same feeling of the hunt. Hence, men are always on the prowl, flirting and looking at every pretty face and shapely woman he sees because he doesn't understand the art of cleaving.

Come off the wall and give him a reason to chase you again. One television commercial that demonstrates this shows the husband/father catching a cab and the children sharing a video they made for him on the advertised phone. The phone's feature is the ability to touch two phones together to transfer the video. They tell him to watch the video when he gets on the plane. Then the wife tells the husband that she made him a video also and touches phones, but tells him that he might not want to look at her video on the plane. The look on his face is one of surprise and excitement. He can't wait to get home to that woman and cleave.

Don't wait for your husband to remember that he is supposed to pursue and cleave to you; must help him, using your own creativity. Bring the God designed excitement back into your marriage. As I mentioned earlier and will fully explain in the next chapter, sex is primarily designed for women but it is designed so that the man will forever desire his wife. She must never make the process of being with her a chore that is so difficult to accomplish that he would rather watch television, play a game or be with the boys.

Make him understand that you want him to cleave and he will embrace the concept with the same desire he had when he first met you!

Happy Cleaving!

Chapter 7: Sex is Primarily for Women

I know nothing about sex,
because I was always
married.

~Zsa Zsa Gabor

ഇ)രു

After the chapter on the womb and the information about sex found in it, you could think I am obsessed with the subject. I'm not obsessed with it; this subject is so under-taught in our churches today that it needs to be a little over done here.

Our young ladies in the church are confused, along with the young men, about why they can't engage in a sexual relationship outside of marriage.

This confusion is due to sex being taught from a wrong focal point. When sex is centered on the needs of men, you then will have a very cut and dry mental approach to the experience.

But with women, the entire experience is tied to her heart keeping emotional excitement attached to the experience.

In the chapter on the womb, I made the case that God designed the woman's womb to clearly indicate that sex is primarily focused on her pleasure. In the chapter on cleaving, it is clear that men should always pursue their wives and this has a great deal to do with sex. Remember, he should be chasing her because she is the good thing found.

Proverbs 18:22 Whoso findeth a wife findeth a good thing, and obtaineth favour of the LORD.

If my premise is correct and sex is primarily designed for women, then there is a new responsibility and attitude that they must embrace that says there is no low hanging fruit!
In other words, it isn't easy and I'm not easy in any way. Sex is not free; you must be completely committed to me in the form of giving your life for me.

This is the reason sex is designed for marriage, because this is the only way you can have a true sense that the man has fully committed his life to you.

I have spoken to so many women who allowed a man who declared his love and affection for them to lure them into sex as a virgin. The majority of these women no longer know where this man is on the earth. Once their hymen, which carries the blood seal for the marriage given to them by God to keep and protect is broken, their hearts are forever connected to this person, even after the man is no longer in their lives.

It wasn't that the man was so experienced or exciting; it was the fact that her heart and her womb are connected.

The first sexual experience where the hymen is broken can be an undercurrent of emotion for women in all of the romantic relationships that come after this encounter. It is my belief that this loss has caused many women to harden their hearts toward men.

Then there is the spirit of lust that is so prominent in this generation that it has caused women to act more like men than women. They are pursuing men, making proposals to men, and even proposing marriage.

Lust has women using their sexuality and their womb as bait to get what they want. DEVALUED!

Young women watch the entertainers in the current culture demonstrate this looseness on television, in movie theaters and through music and want to model themselves after them.

Things such as masturbation have exponentially increased among women over the last ten years. According to the Janus Report on Sexual Behavior[1] and the face to face interview by the author of the Social Organization of sexuality[2], women are catching up with men in this area.

---

[1]Samuel S Janus and Cynthia L Janus , The Janus Report on Sexual Behavior (John Wiley & Sons Inc, 1994)

[2]Edward O. Laumann, John H. Gagnon, Robert T. Michael, Stuart Michaels, The Social Organization of Sexuality (University of Chicago Press, 2000)

The reports indicate that 42% of women and 63% of men have regular masturbating practices. There are many factors for this rise, but the one I am trying to get women to see that sex through love was created so that they would understand their full value. Sex in any other form takes away the value from those it was intended to value.

Sex is not a carrot that should be used to get one's own way or things desired. Neither is sex a free gift that is given because someone asks for it.

Think Special, Live Special

Sex is a very precious and important part of the marital relationship and God gave a major part of the stewardship of it to the woman. It is sad to say that women have not been very good stewards of this precious gift.

Yes, I believe sex is primarily for women, but I also believe that women are responsible for protecting and even helping men understand its importance. When a woman cheapens herself, she looks awful to men and women.

Remember, the woman was created from the side of the man and the man was made from dirt. She was so special to God that He wouldn't even create her from dirt. Therefore, a dirty looking and acting woman is completely out of place with her designed purpose.

It is very easy to be attractive without showing all of the goods. A man who can see the goods doesn't go into the cleaving mode; he goes into the hunting mode.

Once he becomes the hunter you are devalued. When the focal point of the man's attention is your face and eyes he will be closer to cleaving. When breasts and thighs become the focal point, he becomes the hunter.

I see so many beautiful women advertising the merchandise who want to be respected and not treated like a sexual object. These women don't understand what happens in the mind of a man when she reveals her body to him in any way.

I've taught my daughters the mentality of men for their entire lives because men don't think anything like women. Women many times think the men around them think like they do and find the outfit they are wearing cute. But men are only interested in peeking down the blouse or up the skirt and lusting over the revealed shape because the dress is so tight it shows him what he wants to see. He only cares about what is under the outfit. His next thought is how he can get the woman to take the outfit off. He is envisioning the woman naked and the wrong outfit is helping this process.

He can't remember or even care about the color, quality or where the outfit was purchased. Most men have a mental x-ray vision anyway so when a woman dresses loose he is greatly aided and he loves that.

A woman that dresses in a professional or self-respectful manner will also capture a man's attention and he will approach her much differently than the loosely dressed woman. She demands his respect just by how she looks and carries herself.

I know there are some men who are just lustful and would flirt with a nun in her habit without any reservation. But even then your class and eloquence will put him back in his place quickly when you know who you are. So don't allow society to dictate how you should dress or how you view your worth and value. Understand that God values you and created sex so that men would want and value you as well.

Now I hope you can help women who dress loosely understand that what a man views determines his action.

Chapter 8: The Sound That Men Love

જીલ્ડ

"Remember not only to say the right thing in the right place, but far more difficult still, to leave unsaid the wrong thing at the tempting moment."

~Benjamin Franklin

જીલ્ડ

In this chapter, I will unfold what is the kryptonite to most men and causes them to do what they don't want to do. I tell women that they can get the men in their lives to perform the way they have always desired.

The idea of this excites women when it is presented, but they don't realize that it requires them to relearn some very important principles.

We can return to the sexual experience to set the foundation for this principle. When a husband and wife engage in intercourse, the woman can make sounds of passion that completely excites the man.

This doesn't work the same if the man makes all types of sounds. Therefore it is clear that the ears of men can be a way to his heart.

The main key in this chapter is to learn how to take the sound made in passion outside of the bedroom into everyday life. During my *True Value of a Woman* meetings, when I project a picture of puppies on the screen all of the women say, "Oooh," without being prompted. Then I will project a picture of a new born baby on the screen and the sound changes to "Ahhh," but the attitude is the same.

Their reaction to these images provides me with the opportunity to instruct the audience that they are completely aware of the sound and how to make it, but they might not know when or for whom to make it.

When the woman is standing in front of the man announcing purpose it positions her as the help meet to make the proper sound. The sound that causes the man to become compliant and weak in his resolve is one that affirms him and supports him.

Stop Facing Him

Women have turned from their position of announcing to one of confrontation. This is not the sound that will cause men to move in a positive way. Since the man is a protector, when he is attacked he must resist the attacker.

Many women believe that is their duty to tell the men in their lives what to do; to tell them what they are doing wrong and when they are complete idiots. But doing this will completely backfire in most cases. I would agree that there are areas where men really need help and instruction, but it is the way they are told that will create a change in the man.

If it doesn't provoke an argument, the man will shut down and will have nothing to say. This can cause another confrontation when the woman tries to get him to explain his silence. All of this could have been avoided but it takes a woman who is secure in herself and wise enough to know that she wants results and not someone to tell her that she was right.

I have instructed women with a son to speak to him in the proper way and he will do everything in his power to please her. Men hate to hear fussing and complaining! But there isn't a man on the planet that hates praise and supportive words.

You might be asking the question, "Does making the proper sound really work?" Here we go back to the sex issue again, but men are completely fooled by a woman making sounds of passion even if there is no passion. An old woman on one end of a phone making sounds of passion while sitting in an office reading a book can have a man on the other end running over with excitement. There are men who call these sexual chat services just to hear the sound of passion and pleasure.

When I teach this principle of the sound to men they are all shaking their heads up and down in affirmation. In men's meetings I make the argument that pornography is watched more for the sound than the images seen.

There are many different types of woman involved in pornography but after awhile there is nothing new to see so why do men keep watching? It is because of the sound! A man gets excited when he hears the sound of pleasure coming from a woman even if it is connected to someone else. He is also excited when he hears the sound when it has nothing to do with sex.

What Does This Sound Like?

Men will visit the same place of business daily because a woman in the place uses words of endearment to address him. There is no real flirting or relationship, just a woman who knows how to get repeat customers.

The woman in the office tells the man that his tie is nice and goes well with is outfit. She moves on to her area of responsibility thinking nothing about the statement, but her statement left an impact in the heart of the man. Soon after this encounter, the man's spouse asks him why he wears that tie to work so often.

 It is because of the compliment coming from a woman who admired the tie. But his wife says, "Why are you wearing that ugly tie, and are you really wearing those pants?" Well you get the picture!

Believe me that men will move positively toward the right sound and quickly away from sounds of negativity. It would appear that a man's heart is more connected to his ears and his ears want to hear a woman happy and experiencing pleasure more than anything. This is why angry, bitter, debating and complaining women are often alone. This type of woman blames men for being uninterested in her but her mouth is not seasoned to attract his ears.

Colossians 4:6 Let your speech be always with grace, seasoned with salt, that ye may know how ye ought to answer every man.

Romans 10:17 So then faith cometh by hearing, and hearing by the word of God.

When a man takes time to purchase a gift for the woman in his life he does so to hear the sound. The woman can completely mess this up if she makes it about the gift. The wise woman will forever be showered with gifts because she has learned what sound to make and when to make the sound.

I've instructed women to never make the sound that indicates pleasure and excitement about things that they don't truly feel that way about in an attempt not to disappoint the men in their lives. Women who have made this mistake have received many of the same types of gifts from their men because they believe the gift made them happy once so why wouldn't it work again.

On the other hand the woman can't make him feel stupid about his purchase. So what should she do when he purchases something that is absolutely horrible but he purchased it to hear the sound.

Give him the sound and instruction without destroying your chances of getting other gifts. If you handle this situation wrong your gifts from this man will vanish. If you make a big deal about the fact he would take his time to get you a gift and how much you love him for that then instruction can be given about what you like and how you like it.

Immediately follow up the instruction with words that make him feel special for thinking about you!

Mothers and Sons

If you want your son to take the trash out when the can is full or to do any other chore all that is needed are words of affirmation.

> Mother: "I am so happy when you take the trash out!"

> Son: (Not a word spoken but he takes note in his heart)

To reinforce the action, the son should hear his mother telling someone else about how well he performs the task of taking out the trash (while he is present or just within hearing distance). You will never have to tell him again to take the trash out. The mother should still periodically exalt him or reward him for doing so.

The phrase "Mama's Boy" comes from the example of a son who is very close to his mother and allows her involvement in his affairs. But how did she gain this place in his heart above just being his mother?

Have you ever heard how this mother speaks with her son? The sound completely pleases his ears and heart. What can be surprising is how she speaks with her husband if she is married. She can sometimes completely miss this principle where her spouse is concerned but the sound is operating regularly and effectively with her son.

Give and Receive

When men hear the things I am telling you in this chapter, they tell me that I shouldn't give away all of our secrets, because every man clearly knows that he can't resist the right sound coming from a woman.

If you think the sounds of complaint, anger, self exaltation, put downs and the like will change the men in your life, then ignore my suggestion.

Women have told me that they need to hear sounds of affirmation as well and that their spouse or boyfriend always puts them down. There are amazing principles in the bible which say, "Give and it shall be given," and if "you show yourself friendly you will have friends."

Give what you want to experience so it will come back greater than you gave it! Start practicing the sound today and begin to enjoy the spoils.

Women have asked, "What should they do if their men don't have anything that is praise worthy"?

My instruction is for them to find something even if it is routine and extremely small to start with and watch him increase from there.

Maybe the only thing that he does well is to return the seat to its proper position after using the bathroom; make a big deal about that. Come out of the bathroom and compliment him for never having to reposition the seat and he will start doing other things without you asking him so that he can hear that sound again.

When you are doing what I am outlining in this chapter and the man in your life is continually putting you down and treating you badly then it is time to make serious changes. If you are married get in front of someone who can help him with his anger and impatience as soon as possible. If you are dating this person, run and run fast because there are heart issues that your relationship will not solve.

Most of the time the man with character issues will reveal his hand, but he understands that you have the ability to run so he will apologize in the hope that you will forgive him and move on. This was your clear sign that he has problems so don't overlook this sign or any others like this.

When everything is normal the principle of seed time and harvest will work in relationship to the sound. Speak soft and tender to your man and watch him give you his full attention. Ask him to tell you about what he does for a living; show genuine interest and he will talk about anything else you want. Tell him how much you love being in his life and love the way he treats you. He will do everything in his power to keep you feeling that way.

This is a very powerful tool and shouldn't be used recklessly without regard for people feelings. Don't go around the office controlling men with your sweet affirmations and empty compliments. It could produce more than you really want to handle and label you as a tease. But done with the right motives, your life and relationships will increase where men are concerned.

Learn the sound, use the sound and be the sound!

Section 4: The Covenant

Chapter 9: True Marriage

Today the subject of marriage is greatly debated. A redefinition of marriage seems to be the focus and goal of many in society. It is clear that the family structure will suffer if this agenda is accomplished but I believe the main people who will suffer are women.

Remember that a man should cleave to the woman and they two shall become one flesh. The principle of cleaving was designed for marriage and not dating so that the woman would always experience and know her value.

In the redefining of marriage men want to marry each other taking the woman out of the picture. And when two women want to marry each other the one designed to cleave (the man) is removed from this process. The people involved in these relationships have one major problem. They cannot give themselves the internal wiring necessary to really imitate the marriage relationship between a man and woman. It takes a man and woman to trigger the internal programming for this functionality to be engaged.

Watch Out for the Dirt!

God told Adam to search among the animals to find a help meet and he found nothing that could function in worship the way he did. When God created the woman and presented her to Adam, he knew that she was perfect and perfectly designed for his completion. Without mother and father, he declared that man should leave his parents to join to his wife.

Genesis 2:23, 24 And Adam said, This is now bone of my bones, and flesh of my flesh: she shall be called Woman, because she was taken out of Man. ²⁴Therefore shall a man leave his father and his mother, and shall cleave unto his wife: and they shall be one flesh.

The process of their creation was totally different; the man was fashioned from the clay and the woman was created from his side.

This says to me that the woman was not to be associated with dirt. Have you ever been around a woman who curses regularly, and noticed that it didn't sit well with your heart or ears?

Men who curse aren't held to the same standard and it doesn't disturb the listener as much. Many times I heard women complain about things men do, that if they would do the same thing they are considered loose or dirty.

God never intended for the woman to do the things men do. If He wanted her to be dirty, He would have created her from the dirt. So it is important that you think of yourself in the way God presented you to Adam, in all of your beauty and splendor.

Men Love Dirt

As a woman, you must be very careful that you aren't pulled into the dirty world and mind of men. Most fashions are created by men who design clothes that reveal the woman's body in ways that cause her to embrace the dirt.

I can hear some of your thoughts, and you need to understand that even if the designer is a woman, she can be influenced by the desires of the masculine mindset.

Men have persuaded women to enter their dirty world of pornography, prostitution and internet exposure. All of these things help satisfy his desires for sex and fulfill his dirty mind, but they shouldn't be for you.

Today's cultural attitudes are so entangled in the minds of today's women that many women think that they have made an independent decision to embrace the dirt.

But it is much like a frog in water: if you place him in hot water he will quickly jump out, but if you place him in cold water and slowly bring up the heat, he will sit there and cook to death.

This is the way hell has invaded the culture and changed the designed purpose of God for all of society, but especially for women. Remember, the enemy hates the womb because Jesus entered the world through the womb, destroyed Satan's works and freed the world.

Luke 1:15, 16 For he shall be great in the sight of the Lord, and shall drink neither wine nor strong drink; and he shall be filled with the Holy Ghost, even from his mother's womb. ¹⁶And many of the children of Israel shall he turn to the Lord their God.

Luke 2:21
And when eight days were accomplished for the circumcising of the child, his name was called JESUS, which was so named of the angel before he was conceived in the womb.

One Person, One Name

Have you noticed I have not called the original woman's name?
Now that we are clear on the order and importance of the woman's creation, we can better understand how she is connected to the man in oneness.

Adam called her "Woman," which gives her purpose based on the designer, God. It was Adam who named the animals because he understood their purpose. It is no different with the woman; when he saw her he could name her because of the purpose she would fulfill.

If you are a woman reading this book, you know that you are a woman but it is not acceptable to refer to you by that term alone, as in, "Hey Woman!"

Most will reply, "This woman has a name!"
You are a woman aren't you? Yes, but that is an impersonal term and it doesn't distinguish between you and other women.

So, did Adam go around referring to his wife as woman? What was her name? Did you reply, "Eve?"

Sorry to inform you, but that is not correct. I know it is what they taught in Sunday school and it is the name you hear anytime some refers to the first couple.

Because Adam and Eve is all that is taught, the true understanding of marriage has been attacked and even in many ways lost.

What I am about to show you, which has been in the bible for centuries, will completely strengthen marriage and remove all of the doubt.

Genesis 5:1, 2 This is the book of the generations of Adam. In the day that God created man, in the likeness of God made he him; [2]Male and female created he them; and blessed them, and called their name Adam, in the day when they were created.

It was for this reason that I started the book explaining the fact that God spoke with them and blessed them. And notice what they were called "Adam".

Mr. and Mrs. Adam became one in the garden, and out of their oneness they worshipped the Lord. There is no way to become one except that someone receives the name of another.

When God came down in the cool of the day and called Adam they both came and communed with Him. This is clearer once the fall happens and God calls for Adam but not for his wife.

Genesis 3:9 And the LORD God called unto Adam, and said unto him, Where art thou?

But now we know He was calling them both using the one name that identified them, "Adam". It wasn't until the disobedience that the woman's name was changed to Eve. The principle associated with covenant is that when a covenant is established names are changed to indicate the oneness and when covenants are broken names are also changed.

114

After the fall there a separation occurs in the garden and now there are two people instead of one perfect person. Since the woman would be the mother of all who would live, Adam called her Eve.

When Abraham enters the covenant with God his name was Abram and God added "ah" to his name. His wife's name was Sarai and God changed her name to Sarah adding the same "ah" to her name. What was done with the man was also done with his wife.

Each time a marriage covenant is established a name change must occur with it.

The reason the two have to become one is so that a new creature can be formed. When a man and woman come together in marriage, a creature that has not existed before is created.

Most have not recognized that three different human creatures fill the earth. A man, a woman and a man & woman who have become one in marriage; these are the three human creatures filling the earth.

The Miracle Overlooked

If you have ever attended a wedding, then the third creature was formed right in front of your eyes. It is a miracle of God's hand to take two and make them one without changing their physical features and allowing them to walk the earth as two individuals.

Adam understood that this new creature of oneness would be created from the moment Mrs. Adam was presented to him after her creation.

Genesis 2:24 Therefore shall a man leave his father and his mother, and shall cleave unto his wife: and they shall be one flesh.

It is worth restating that the woman is not only this creature, who can produce children and replenish the earth, but she is completely capable of advancing the vision and purposes of God on the earth. She is not the appendix of the man, she is his completion and their agreement and focus is very difficult to stop when they decide to take ground.

Men who can have the desert without paying for the meal will do so as much as possible this is another reason why premarital intercourse must not be something you would ever consider.

Like the frog in water, since women were slowly convinced that having children without the covenant agreement with the man was okay, they have suffered loss. The man is gone to sow his oats in other fields while the woman is left to take care of and raise the child alone.

I understand that the woman loves her child, but who actually came out best in this deal?

In the marriage that God designed, a woman is never devalued. The children come forth from the union to help to increase it and to honor the father and the mother. The family structure is designed to show even more value to the woman, wife and mother!

Fathers should teach their sons how to respect and honor their mothers and sisters since they will need this training when a wife is joined to him. Daughters should be taught how to celebrate their fathers and brothers so that they will have a head start on understanding the benefits of the sound.

When the household has a healthy worship relationship then every family member can experience the greatness of God and the children can make this a part of their lives once they leave their parent's home.

This is just one of the reasons that the rippling effect of divorce causes so much pain. God said that man didn't have the right to separate what He had put together in His infinite wisdom.

Every time divorce takes place Satan is sitting over in the corner of the court room or in the lawyer's office with a big smile on his face. God's design is being destroyed and the power that two who became one can produce is now no more.

Ecclesiastes 4:9, 10 Two are better than one; because they have a good reward for their labour. [10]For if they fall, the one will lift up his fellow: but woe to him that is alone when he falleth; for he hath not another to help him up.

Turn and Face the Audience

Once the wedding ceremony is concluded it is the responsibility of the officiant to announce the new couple. In my case my wife walked down the aisle with her father as Joanndra Forbes but when Bishop Wellington and Mrs. Boone announced us to the audience they said, Mr. and Mrs. Larry A. Jackson.

My wife didn't take my last name as it is understood but she took my full name and I became a Mrs., even though I am not a female. A person who was not in the service at the beginning of the ceremony has now been announced to the audience.

True marriage is between creatures that are different from one another so that a new creature can be formed. Adding two creatures together that are the same can increase the numbers of the creature, but will not make it different.

Only a man and woman can create the third human being that walks this earth, and God has declared a blessing over their lives.

The church has also embraced another custom put forth by the world of the woman using a hyphen to keep her father's name and identity. A new creature isn't announced when this practice is embraced. The man can't become one with the woman's father.

Remember, their name was Adam in the day they were created. Not Adam and Eve! Your father could be a very blessed man and provided well for you, but a person and vision is being established on the earth that isn't dependent upon your father's involvement.

No one can see the third person walking down the aisle with the couple but it is Jesus and He can do what your father could never do. I instruct couples that a true marriage consists of three people and not just two.

The purpose of the marriage is so the couple can show worth to their creator for the life and vision given them. In the ceremonies I conduct the couple receives communion before they salute each other so that they can acknowledge Jesus before they acknowledge each other in a moment of intimacy.

From this day the couple should never forgot the third person and always include Him (Jesus) in their lives and decisions.

Chapter 10: The GOOD Thing Found

 C3&O

What a happy and holy
fashion it is that those who
love one another should rest on
the same pillow.

~Nathaniel Hawthorne

&)CR

What I will share in this chapter causes a lot of women to challenge or outright reject the information. Before I go there, let's look at the scripture that inspired the chapter title.

*Proverbs 18:22 Whoso findeth a wife findeth a **good thing**, and obtaineth favour of the LORD.*

It is my guess that we don't have a debate about the scripture and its importance. Every man who finds a wife should understand this passage and follow its principle.

Let's look at another scripture that is a companion passage to Proverbs 18:22.

Proverbs_12:4 A virtuous woman is a crown to her husband:

These are two lovely scriptures, but I believe they aren't being followed, and in many cases, not even considered.

Because they aren't, the value that should be placed on the woman has all but vanished out of society as well as out of the church.

In Proverbs 18 a powerful principle is presented: it is the man who finds the wife and not the woman who finds the husband.

When he positions himself to propose to, provide for, and protect the woman even before she is his wife, then the same should hold true after the wedding.

She is the valued thing in this picture. Once she is found, the Lord favors him because he has found his completeness and a new creature is formed that will produce what the two apart could never accomplish.

She is so precious that the bible declares that she is a crown to her husband. Crowns show the world that one with authority is coming or is already on the scene.

This crown can very well represent the woman being out in front announcing the purposes of their union. One thing we are sure of is that it is beautiful, and very costly.

The question I ask the women in my meetings, with these facts in mind is, "Who is the wedding designed for?" They have problems with the answer In the same way as when I ask men who is sex designed for.

First, let me ask another question. Who was found and who did the finding?

If I found treasure in a field, wouldn't it make sense that you would congratulate me and not the treasure? The entire care for the treasure would rest solely on me, but I was the one who became better for finding it.

If there was a party because of my discovery, would it be for me or the treasure? Then why is it that in North America, women think the good thing found should control the wedding process?

Mothers and daughters have thought about and planned the wedding from the daughter's childhood, without ever looking at its true design and purpose.

The wedding is designed for the woman to be honored and valued, by the one who found her and everyone in their lives.

By far, he is not an appendix in this process; it is his process. Remember, this is all done to model Christ and the church. The church understands that there will be a wedding and marriage someday, but has absolutely no idea of the date or place where it will be held.

The duty of the woman is to find a wedding dress that will make her look beautiful so that she will be ready when her man comes for her.

Then shall the kingdom of heaven be likened unto ten virgins, which took their lamps, and went forth to meet the bridegroom. [2]And five of them were wise, and five were foolish. [3]They that were foolish took their lamps, and took no oil with them: [4]But the wise took oil in their vessels with their lamps. [5]While the bridegroom tarried, they all slumbered and slept. [6]And at midnight there was a cry made, Behold, the bridegroom cometh; go ye out to meet him. [7]Then all those virgins arose, and trimmed their lamps. [8]And the foolish said unto the wise, Give us of your oil; for our lamps are gone out. [9]But the wise answered, saying, Not so; lest there be not enough for us and you: but go ye rather to them that sell, and buy for yourselves. [10]And while they went to buy, the bridegroom came; and they that were ready went in with him to the marriage: and the door was shut. [11]Afterward came also the other virgins, saying, Lord, Lord, open to us. [12]But he answered and said, Verily I say unto you, I know you not. [13]Watch therefore, for ye know neither the day nor the hour wherein the Son of man cometh. [14]For the kingdom of heaven is as a man travelling into a far country, who called his own servants, and delivered unto them his goods. [15]And unto one he gave five talents, to another two, and to another one; to every man according to his several ability; and straightway took his journey. Matthew 25:1-13

I understand that men aren't going to become wedding planners, but they should not be shut out of the decision making process. The reason we have something called a "bridezilla" is because the woman thinks it is all about her.

It *is* about her, but not in the way she thinks. Therefore, even though he loves her enough to marry her, she hasn't allowed him to honor and value her at the level he should.

It is not the mother of the bride's wedding day either. She should have little or nothing to say in this process. That might sound cruel, but it is biblical. By the way, my mother-in-law didn't interfere in my wedding, so I am not telling you this out of any kind of bitterness.

When you follow kingdom standards, many things that we do will come under attack so that they can be adjusted for the purpose of presenting them to the world correctly. Believe me I've been challenged on this principle and had to adjust my delivery of it so that it would be better received. I want you to enjoy your wedding day and the planning process but don't leave the man out.

Gave Himself

The bible tells the husband that his wife is so valued and precious that he is to give his life for her!

Husbands, love your wives, even as Christ also loved the church, and gave himself for it; That he might sanctify and cleanse it with the washing of water by the word, That he might present it to himself a glorious church, not having spot, or wrinkle, or any such thing; but that it should be holy and without blemish. So ought men to love their wives as their own bodies. He that loveth his wife loveth himself. For no man ever yet hated his own flesh; but nourisheth and cherisheth it, even as the Lord the church: For we are members of his body, of his flesh, and of his bones. Ephesians 5:25-30

The man who truly understands that his wife is one with him, will do everything in his power to make her happy.

He found her and convinced her to leave the security of her family to join him in name and purpose. It follows the pattern set by Jesus with the church; He has told her that anything asked in His name He will do.

Jesus came to the earth and found us, we didn't find Him; that indicates He placed a value on us. He then gave His life to pay the dowry cost set by the Father to have our hand in marriage. The cost was great, but Jesus believed it was worth the price to make us one with Him.

You see, the true marriage has to do with Christ and His church and not just a man and a woman. With all of the things man is attempting to do to change the designed pattern of marriage, they can't touch the true marriage.

Those of us who follow the kingdom agenda understand that marriage has far more to do with Jesus than with people finding love on the earth. Therefore, if we are going to have a successful marriage, it will take three people instead of two. It will take the man, the woman, and Jesus as the third and most important person; because it is through Him that everything is held together.

The man and woman are not seen as two separate people, but as one person (The Church/Wife) who now serves the Lord Jesus Christ (Husband).

Always remember the value Jesus placed on those who would become the church, and expect that same value to be placed on you as a potential bride.

In the wedding receiving line the people should congratulate the husband and express how beautiful the bride is. This is because he found his good thing in his wife and his life has just increased and the beautiful woman on his arm has made him look so much better.

In the next chapter I will outline the way Jesus is marrying the church and all of the steps he is taking that places increased value on his bride (the church).

If Jesus is following this pattern how much more should a woman allow her man to do the same?

Enjoy your wedding but always remember whose wedding it really is, the husband's!

Section 5: Single Women Guide

Chapter 11: True Love

ᐸᔓᐳ

A single woman, of good fortune, is always respectable, and may be as sensible and pleasant as anybody else."

~Jane Austen, Emma

ᔓᐳᐸ

Most of the references in this book have been toward married women, so this chapter is dedicated to give a few answers to the single woman.

Making sense of relationships, careers, social pressures and age can cause the single woman a great deal of anxiety.

It for this reason the single woman must understand the importance of staying in the word of the Lord and being before Him in worship.

Many single women have told me that they need more than just reading and prayer, they need companionship. It is this need that has caused problems in the lives of so many lovely ladies. Because of the loneliness of their hearts they open their lives to pain that can linger for years and years.

I have five daughters, and three are still single and of marrying age. We have talked about the needs and desires of their hearts from a natural and spiritual point of view. As their father, it is my job to instruct and guide them into the best possible situation for their lives' success.

One thing I help them see is the fact that loneliness has never killed anyone. It is only a state of mind! The lonely person in most cases has not developed a deep, intimate relationship with the Lord.

Single men and women will always counter this statement by telling me about how much time they read their bibles and pray. It is great that these disciplines are found in the lives of single Christians, but it doesn't always create a close personal relationship.

These things can be done as part of a Christian checklist and not because of a passion for the Lord. The prayer list can be a "give me list" instead of a "what do you want of me?" list.

Matthew 6:33 But seek ye first the kingdom of God, and his righteousness; and all these things shall be added unto you.

Notice that the things will be added <u>after</u> we seek His righteousness. God wants each of us to be happy, but He wants us to stay on the proper road.

Your single life will help you prepare for the time when a man declares that you are the good thing found. Develop that with Jesus now in this time where it is just you and Him.

First Love

Isaiah 54:5 For thy Maker is thine husband; the LORD of hosts is his name; and thy Redeemer the Holy One of Israel; The God of the whole earth shall he be called.

Many Christian singles today are often consumed by the desire for a marriage partner. In the American dream, the ideal life begins when you find a husband or wife. There are women who feel they can never be fulfilled as a woman unless they have a husband. There is some truth to those feelings, but they are looking for the wrong husband. The bible says that our Maker is our husband, and He marries those who are a part of His church. The church is Jesus' bride and it is the one He is coming back for. Every Christian is to be married first to God. Jesus is to be our First Love.

Christians often resist the advances of their First Love when they have never truly yielded their affections to Him. Jesus told the church at Ephesus, "I have somewhat

against thee, because thou has left thy first love."
Revelation 2:4

In the *Message*, Jesus' words are these:

"I see what you've done, your hard, hard work, your refusal to quit. I know you can't stomach evil, that you weed out apostolic pretenders. I know your persistence, your courage in my cause that you never wear out."

"But you walked away from you first love—why? What's going on with you, anyway? Do you have any idea how far you've fallen? A Lucifer fall!"

"Turn back! Recover your dear early love. No time to waste" (Revelation 2, MNT, p. 516).

The more vital our prayer lives become, the more our lives are filled with worship. God becomes so attractive that we can hardly stay away from Him. We are overtaken by His beauty. When we call, God answers. He knows us in complete intimacy. When we enter into His presence, we are filled with thanksgiving and praise because He loves us.

"And I will betroth thee unto me forever, yea, I will betroth thee unto me in righteousness, and in judgment, and in lovingkindness, and in mercies. I will even betroth thee unto me in faithfulness: and thou shalt know the Lord."
Hosea 2:19-20

Those who leave their First Love have never developed a true marriage intimacy with God in the prayer closet, and therefore have problems in serving Him as His loving bride. Just as in human marriage between a man and a woman, the quality of the relationship depends on the quality of the intimacy. Jesus said, "But thou, when thou prayest, enter into thy closet, and when thou hast shut thy door, pray to thy Father which is in secret shall reward thee openly." *Matthew 6:6*

Jesus discussed intimacy with God one day when the religious hypocrites gathered around to try to trap Him. They described a woman who had died and gone to heaven. Since she had been married to seven husbands, they asked who would be her husband at the resurrection of the dead. Here is His response (in two versions of the Bible):

"And Jesus answering said unto them, Do ye not therefore err, because ye know not the scriptures, neither the power of God? For when they shall rise from the dead, they neither marry, nor are given in marriage; but are as the angels which are in heaven." Mark 12:24-25 KJV

"Jesus said, "You're way off base, and here's why: One, you don't know your Bibles; two, you don't know how God works. After the dead are raised up, we're past the marriage business. As it is with angels now, all our ecstasies and intimacies then will be with God." Mark 12, The Message, p. 101

Do you understand what Jesus was saying? He rebuked them for their spiritual dullness to the Scriptures and the priorities of God, and He used the occasion to give them a proper perspective on marriage. He identified for them their true and eternal marriage partner, God Himself.

The bible says that, individually and corporately, believers are married to God. "For thy maker is thine husband; the Lord of hosts is his name, and thy redeemer the Holy One of Israel." *Isaiah 54:5*

The church today needs a fresh perspective on marriage. Human marriage is not wrong, and this manual will tell you how to make it work, but it is something that is limited to life in the realm of earth.

If you search for the right mate because of increasing age, feelings of loneliness, or a response to another person's desire for you, you are missing the eternal calling of God on your individual life. Singles must develop a perspective on marriage that is based upon revelation.

Marry someone if God calls you to do so, but never let this person interfere with your First Love. If you love God first, you will really love your mate. You will be fulfilled before you ever meet this person, and so your relationship with your marriage partner will be extraordinarily blessed.

Most singles have a confused vision for marriage that is an unstable mixture of cultural pressures and a shallow understanding of the mind of God. The world's godless programming continually bombards us, telling us that an attractive, sexually fulfilling mate is the answer to our emptiness. In the church, many single Christians waste precious mental and emotional energy being driven by their perceived need for marriage in order to cultivate an intimate relationship with a mate. However, a relationship with God is the best guarantee of a fulfilled marriage.

Know ye not that the friendship of the world is enmity with God? whosoever therefore will be a friend of the world is the enemy of God. Do ye think that the scripture saith in vain, The spirit that dwelleth in us lusteth to envy? [6] But he giveth more grace. Wherefore he saith, God resisteth the proud, but giveth grace unto the humble.[7] Submit yourselves therefore to God. James 4:4-7

If all you want is your own way, flirting with the world every chance you get, you end up enemies of God and his way. And do you suppose God doesn't care? The proverb has it that "he's a fiercely jealous lover." And what he gives in love is far better than anything else you'll find. It's common knowledge that "God goes against the willful proud; God gives grace to the willing humble."

"So let God work his will in you."James 4, MNT, p. 483

There are some single men and women who don't think I should take this position since I am married. This could be accepted if I came from my mother's womb a married man but I didn't. The thing I am telling you I lived when I became saved and understood God's love for me. I was single and resisted female companionship so that I could fully experience the Father's love. When I found my wife she was so focused o the Lord and her relationship with Him that she turned down my marriage proposal several times prior to saying yes. We did not get married because of worldly pressure but because Father brought us together to fulfill His purpose on the earth.

Already Married!

As the vision of God for your life becomes clearer, and the principles shared in this book become life to you, your appetite for earthly marriage for its own sake will die and it will be replaced with a hunger to lay hold of your destiny in the kingdom of God. Your love for Him will come alive, and your ability to love others will explode.

> "Blessed be the God Father of our Lord Jesus Christ, who hath blessed us with all spiritual blessings in heavenly places in Christ." Ephesians 1:3

> "How blessed is God! And what a blessing he is! He's the Father of our Master, Jesus Christ, and takes us to the high places of blessing in him." Ephesians 1, MNT, P 402

For too long, we have accepted salvation but still desired to live like the world.

> "Wherefore, my beloved brethren, let every man be swift to hear, slow to speak, slow to wrath:
> For the wrath of man worketh not the righteousness of God. Wherefore lay apart all filthiness and superfluity of naughtiness, and receive with meekness the engrafted word, which is able to save your souls." James 1:19-21

*"In simple humility, let our gardener, God, landscape you
with the Word, making a salvation-garden of your life."
James 1, MNT, P. 480*

Before the foundation of the world, we were individually
chosen to be married to Christ.

*"According as he hath chosen us in him before the
foundation of the world, that we should be holy and
without blame before him in love:" Ephesians 1:4*

As you study and mediate on the principles in this book,
steward the call of God in your life. Apply what you read to
your Christian walk, not only in the search for a mate, but
also in your relationship with God.

Jesus is following the Hebraic pattern to marry a woman in
His espousal to the bride (the Church) He came to earth to
receive.

The ancient Hebraic custom in marriage had fourteen
specific parts that all had a direct connection to the value
placed on the woman. These are the things you must look
for and expect before allowing your heart to be given over
to a man just because he shows interest in you or treats
you nicely.

The Betrothal Process

The man is responsible to God to find you; it shouldn't be
the other way around. It is ok to pray for God to lead the

man to the place that he can find you, and since you can fully trust the Lord, you can destroy your checklist.

If anyone should have the checklist, it is the one searching for the treasure, not the treasure!

Ye have not chosen me, but I have chosen you, and ordained you, that ye should go and bring forth fruit, and that your fruit should remain: that whatsoever ye shall ask of the Father in my name, he may give it you. John 15:16

The Arrangement

The father of the bride is very important to the process of keeping the proper value on the woman. If a natural father is not in the picture, a spiritual father or father figure must take his place. One of the major problems with fathers being removed out of society is that it devalues their daughters in the eyes of their pursuers.

The process isn't a dating process but a courtship process, and for it to be done in a proper fashion, a father is needed to speak with the man like a man. Everything that takes place in this process is under the supervision of the father. The daughter at this point has the name of her father and must protect his name at all costs.

Once the bride is chosen, then the two men agree on the price required for the potential bridegroom to have the daughter's hand in marriage.

Notice that she isn't paying the price, the man is! If he is broke, then there is no marriage. They can tell the father all about how much they are in love, but the father must keep the value of his daughter before the eyes of the man. The father knows that what a man has to commit to and purchase carries a greater value in his heart. This is one of the reasons that once the man has pre-marital sex with a woman, he has no other need for her, since what he valued was sex and that is now off of his list. The price agreement secures the fact that this woman isn't going to be touched until she is fully valued.

For you were bought at a price; therefore glorify God in your body and in your spirit, which are God's. 1 Corinthians 6:20

...knowing that you were not redeemed with corruptible things, like silver or gold, from your aimless conduct received by tradition from your fathers, but with the precious blood of Christ, as of a lamb without blemish and without spot. 1 Peter 1:18-19

The Marriage Contract

Next, there is a covenant agreement between the father, the potential bridegroom, and the bride.
The covenant or contract details the husband's obligations to his wife, both in the natural and spiritually. Notice again where the responsibility lies; it is with the husband and not with the wife. When Mrs. Adam was presented to Adam, she had absolutely no needs.

142

For this is my blood of the new covenant, which is shed for many for the remission of sins. Matthew 26:28

For finding fault with them, he saith, Behold, the days come, saith the Lord, when I will make a new covenant with the house of Israel and with the house of Judah: Hebrews 8:8

Not according to the covenant that I made with their fathers in the day when I took them by the hand to lead them out of the land of Egypt; because they continued not in my covenant, and I regarded them not, saith the Lord. Hebrews 8:9

For this is the covenant that I will make with the house of Israel after those days, saith the Lord; I will put my laws into their mind, and write them in their hearts: and I will be to them a God, and they shall be to me a people: Hebrews 8:10

And they shall not teach every man his neighbour, and every man his brother, saying, Know the Lord: for all shall know me, from the least to the greatest. Hebrews 8:11

For I will be merciful to their unrighteousness, and their sins and their iniquities will I remember no more. Hebrews 8:12

In that he saith, A new covenant, he hath made the first old. Now that which decayeth and waxeth old is ready to vanish away. Hebrews 8:13

The Bride's Consent

With all of this done between the potential husband and the father, the woman must still give her consent. She holds all of the power in that if she doesn't want it, then she is covered by her father and the man has no rights to her. Her father can attempt to persuade her but she has the right of refusal. Therefore, no one can force you to give your life to anyone. It is your choice, and you should only do so when you are properly valued and honored the way you want to be.

...if you confess with your mouth the Lord Jesus and believe in your heart that God has raised Him from the dead, you will be saved. Romans 10:9

Drinking From the Cup (sealing the engagement)

This portion of the marriage tradition is very important and should be observed on a regular basis. Most only participate in the sealing of the engagement during the communion service at church, but Jesus told the disciples that they should do this often. It keeps the church aware of the fact that they are already purchased and married.

Likewise he also took the cup after supper, saying, "This cup is the new covenant in my blood, which is shed for you. Luke 22:20

After the same manner also he took the cup, when he had supped, saying, This cup is the new testament in my blood: this do ye, as oft as ye drink it, in remembrance of me. 1Corinthians 11:25

Bride Receives Gift from the Bridegroom

The main gift the man provides for the woman is the ring. Have you thought about the fact that the only one with a gift before the ceremony is the woman? Valued!

The bride doesn't have to wait for gifts at the marriage celebration because the bridegroom honors her by bringing gifts with him before the ceremony.
This is another example of the value placed on the woman that she should be lavished with gifts.

In whim you also trusted, after you heard the word of truth, the gospel of your salvation; in whom also, having believed, you were sealed with the Holy Spirit of promise, who is the guarantee of our inheritance until the redemption of the purchased possession, to the praise of His glory. Ephesians 1:13-14

But the manifestation of the Spirit is given to each one for the profit of all: for to one is given the word of wisdom through the Spirit, to another the word of knowledge through the same Spirit, to another faith by the same Spirit, to another gifts of healings by the same Spirit, to another the working of miracles, to another prophecy, to another discerning of spirits, to another different kinds of tongues, to another the interpretation of tongues. 1 Corinthians 12:7-10

The Washing of the Bride (Sanctification)

This is a very important process that involves the woman only and doesn't require any other person's help. Completely nude, she is to enter a water source that is running or moving. She must submerge her entire body under the water several times and repeat the blessing for immersion.

When the believer repents of their sins (Washing of Water) and is found in Christ (Immersion), then that person has now joined the Christ as His bride.

Then Peter said to them, "Repent, and let every one of you be baptized in the name of Jesus Christ for the remission of sins; and you shall receive the gift of the Holy Spirit. Acts 2:38

Husbands, love your wives, just as Christ also loved the church and gave Himself for her, that He might sanctify and cleanse her with the washing of water by the word, that He might present her to Himself a glorious church, not having spot or wrinkle or any such thing, but that she should be holy and without blemish. Ephesians 5:25-27

146

Bridegroom Prepares a Place

In my Father's house are many mansions; if it were not so, I would have told you. I go to prepare a place for you. And if I go and prepare a place for you, I will come again and receive you to myself; that where I am, there you may be also. John 14:2-3

Many people have wondered why Jesus couldn't stay after the resurrection and set up His kingdom at that time. It would have solved a great deal of problems, since the enemy was defeated, death and the grave was defeated, and mankind could reclaim its rightful place.

Jesus had to leave so the marriage would be completed and to add value to the church (bride) He would marry. It is the husband who goes away to provide for the wife so that she can simply enter into her possession. As I mentioned earlier, the weight of the entire process is on the husband's shoulders because it is his wedding and she is the very valuable crown that he found.

Consecration of the Bride

The bride is set apart for her husband and no one else can lay claim to her. She wears a veil to indicate that she isn't espoused to another and will soon be joined with Him where He is. The church is set apart and is veiled from the world and all of its advancements that entice it to be entangled in worldly affairs.

Therefore, brethren, having boldness to enter the Holiest by the blood of Jesus, by a new and living way which he consecrated for us, through the veil, that is, His flesh, and having a High Priest over the house of God, let us draw near with a true heart in full assurance of faith, having our hearts sprinkled from an evil conscience and our bodies washed with pure water. Let us hold fast the confession of our hope without wavering, for he who promised is faithful. And let us consider one another in order to stir up love and good works, not forsaking the assembling of ourselves together, as is the manner of some, but exhorting one another, and so much the more as you see the day approaching. Hebrews 10:19-25

The Return of the Bridegroom

The bible teaches that Christ will return for His bride the church at the appointed time of the Father. It is the father's responsibility to instruct the bridegroom in the preparation. Once the home meets the standard of the father, the bridegroom can then go to receive his bride into her new home.

And he said unto them, It is not for you to know the times or the seasons, which the Father hath put in his own power. Acts 1:7

Let not your heart be troubled: ye believe in God, believe also in me. In my Father's house are many mansions: if it were not so, I would have told you. I go to prepare a place for you. And if I go and prepare a place for you, I will come again, and receive you unto myself; that where I am, there ye may be also. And whither I go ye know, and the way ye know. John 14:1-4

Therefore, brethren, having boldness to enter the Holiest by the blood of Jesus, by a new and living way which He consecrated for us, through the veil, that is, His flesh, and having a High Priest over the house of God, let us draw near with a true heart in full assurance of faith, having our hearts sprinkled from an evil conscience and our bodies washed with pure water. Let us hold fast the confession of our hope without wavering, for He who promised is faithful. And let us consider one another in order to stir up love and good works, not forsaking the assembling of ourselves together, as is the manner of some, but exhorting one another, and so much the more as you see the Day approaching. Hebrews 10:19-25

In the same way, the church is waiting for the return of Christ and He must wait for the Father to release Him to return. There is some debate on how and when this will happen, but the entire church is sure He is coming for His bride and the wedding ceremony confirms that fact.

The Procession Back to the Father's House

The bridegroom doesn't re-enter the father's house, but stands outside and calls for the bride. She is waiting for his return and is keeping a lamp burning in the window to indicate that. Her bridesmaids help her to get ready and she leaves her father's house and is joined to her husband with torches and oil lambs burning. The bride is placed on a blanket, lifted from the ground, carried, and celebrated by all who witness the parade.

But I would not have you to be ignorant, brethren, concerning them which are asleep, that ye sorrow not, even as others which have no hope. For if we believe that Jesus died and rose again, even so them also which sleep in Jesus will God bring with him. For this we say unto you by the word of the Lord, that we which are alive and remain unto the coming of the Lord shall not prevent them which are asleep. For the Lord himself shall descend from heaven with a shout, with the voice of the archangel, and with the trump of God: and the dead in Christ shall rise first: Then we which are alive and remain shall be caught up together with them in the clouds, to meet the Lord in the air: and so shall we ever be with the Lord. Wherefore comfort one another with these words. 1Thessalonians 4:13-18

These are scriptures that are used mostly at funerals but they are really another part of the wedding ceremony. Once a person is a part of the church, then it doesn't matter if they are dead or alive; they will make the procession from this world to the Father.

"And at midnight a cry was heard: 'Behold, the bridegroom is coming; go out to meet him!' Then all those virgins arose and trimmed their lamps. And the foolish said to the wise, 'Give us some of your oil, for our lamps are going out.' But the wise answered, saying, 'No, lest there should not be

enough for us and you; but go rather to those who sell, and buy for yourselves.' And while they went to buy, the bridegroom came, and those who were ready went in with him to the wedding; and the door was shut. Matthew 25:6-10

If the bride isn't ready and her lamp isn't burning in her window, then she could be left behind!

The Consummation

All of the ceremonial things are exciting and rewarding, but the actual marriage isn't sealed until the two people come together in intercourse. Remember, the woman is holding the blood seal to the marriage.

This is very important to her father because this will also indicate her faithfulness to him and to his name. Usually, the virgin will have her hymen broken and blood will be released, sealing the marriage covenant, but also indicating that she is a virgin. If there is no blood, then the marriage is over and the dowry given to the father must be returned. She must be spotless and pure for the marriage to be complete. This is a seven day process where the couple is separated from the guests. Upon their return, the blood stained sheet is presented to the father of the bride to indicate her faithfulness to him.

Husbands, love your wives, even as Christ also loved the church, and gave himself for it; That he might sanctify and cleanse it with the washing of water by the word, That he might present it to himself a glorious church, not having spot, or wrinkle, or any such thing; but that it should be holy and without blemish. Ephesians 5:25-27

Once the believer has come to know Christ, they must do everything in their power under the direction of the Holy Spirit to remain clean for the bridegroom.

The Marriage Supper

When the couple returns to the guests, they will share another cup of wine.

Let us be glad and rejoice and give Him glory, for the marriage of the Lamb has come, and His wife has made herself ready." Revelation 19:7

But I say to you, I will not drink of this fruit of the vine from now on until that day when I drink it new with you in My Father's kingdom." Matthew 26:29

There are many who have indicated that it is okay to drink a little wine even once you have become a Christian, and many do. I have always held the position that if Jesus isn't going to drink again until I am one with Him, then I will not allow any wine or strong drink to enter my mouth either.

I want the wedding ceremony to be completed in the way He has designed it to be.

As you can see, if you are a Christian then you are already in the process of being married. If you are only looking for the man who can fulfill your needs, then you are most likely not focusing on the needs of the Lord.

What I have discovered is that when my focus is on the things concerning Jesus, He will take care of the things concerning me. Jesus wants us to marry so that the world can see the way He loves us through our demonstration of love for each other.

He wants to be your first love and then He will provide your mate.

Section 6: The Movement

Chapter 12: Naomi and Ruth

The previous chapter was primarily written to the single woman but has much to say about the value of all women. This chapter is designed to help women in their lifelong pursuits in any area of life.

While reading the book of Ruth for an annual women's celebration in our church in Charlotte, NC, I discovered a principle that should be pursued after and followed forever.

The reason this principle should be established is because it should be in every person's life; men and women need to make sure they are all functioning from this principled place.

Whenever you find someone who is in constant trouble or who can't seem to make sense out of life, you will find that they have violated this principle. Solomon spoke of this principle many times in the Proverbs as a way to become successful, but too many believers have taken it for granted.

Marriages have failed all over the earth just because this principle, that each person in the marriage should follow, has not been followed due to busy lifestyles, neglect or ignorance of the fact they need it.

What is it, you ask?

It is mentoring and counseling.

For by wise counsel thou shalt make thy war: and in multitude of counsellors there is safety. Proverbs 24:6

Without counsel purposes are disappointed: but in the multitude of counsellors they are established. Proverbs 15:22

Thou therefore, my son, be strong in the grace that is in Christ Jesus. [2]And the things that thou hast heard of me among many witnesses, the same commit thou to faithful men, who shall be able to teach others also. 2 Timothy 2:1, 2

You not only must have a counselor, but the bible indicates that you need many counselors.

These are not just people whom you call mentors, but people you discuss major decisions with. They help when there are setbacks in life and rejoice with you over the victories.

This mentor should be a very sound and level headed person who will not get too high when things go well or will not get too low when things go wrong.

That is what Naomi was for Ruth!

Naomi was the mother-in-law to Ruth and Orpah, two women from Moab who married her two sons.
After the death of her sons, Naomi told the women to return to their native land so that they could find new husbands and live out their lives.

The conversation she had with the two women tells us a great deal about Naomi and the relationship she had with the women. She couldn't have been a mother-in-law who was in competition with her sons' wives. She had a mother/daughter relationship with these women and they didn't want to leave her after the death of their husbands.

In the sitcom "The Jefferson's," George Jefferson's mother was never a mother to his wife Louise. To her, George was always right and she was in constant competition with Louise.

If George Jefferson had died before his mother on the show, there would have been no way Louise would have had anything to do with his mother.

But that wasn't the way it was with Naomi and her two daughters-in-law. Even when she told them to leave they resisted, and even though Orpah finally gave in and returned home, Ruth stayed with Naomi.

And Ruth said, Intreat me not to leave thee, or to return from following after thee: for whither thou goest, I will go; and where thou lodgest, I will lodge: thy people shall be my people, and thy God my God: Where thou diest, will I die, and there will I be buried: the LORD do so to me, and more also, if ought but death part thee and me. When she saw that she was stedfastly minded to go with her, then she left speaking unto her. Ruth 1:16-18

Naomi had become a mentor to Ruth and she wasn't about to let that go. This proves very valuable once they return to Naomi's home town of Bethlehem Judah and Ruth asks to go out to glean the fields so that they would have food.

While she was in the fields working, Boaz, kinsman of Naomi's deceased husband Elimelech, saw Ruth and provided extra gleaning opportunities for her. He was very wealthy and very interested in Ruth, but she was only there because Naomi told her to be.

It is apparent from these scriptures that Ruth was an attractive woman, but Boaz told her that she found grace in his eyes for the way she stayed with Naomi to look after her. The way she valued their relationship impressed his heart.

Most women don't realize that men hate hearing women argue and fuss. Actually, no complaining, confusion and words of bitterness sound good in the ears of a man. We don't even like it when a woman is having problems with another woman. I think it all goes back to the fact that women aren't made from dirt! And men want to hear the proper sound coming from women and it is not the sound of anger and confusion.

When men hear of women getting along and having respect for each other, this really pleases their hearts. This made Ruth even more attractive in the eyes of Boaz and he wasn't going to let this woman get away.

When she told Naomi about the favor she found with Boaz and how the fields were open to more gleaning, Naomi instructed her how to position herself so that the other women wouldn't become jealous of her while accomplishing her task.

This could have become a major problem had the women who had eyes for Boaz not wanted the new girl to glean more than them, or if their dislike caused them to attack her and make her feel uncomfortable.

The wisdom of Naomi helped Ruth understand how to move through this potential mine field so that the other women wouldn't dislike her, and everything progressed just fine. That is what a mentor should do; they should help keep you from potential problems. Once the information or instructions are given, you must listen, even when you don't necessarily agree.

It was Naomi who instructed Ruth how to position herself and capture the heart of Boaz. Ruth followed her instruction to the letter, and it caught Boaz's attention without Ruth having to compromise her standards.

Many women will attempt to deal with men that are attractive to them by themselves and that can be a mistake. Notice that there was no need for Ruth to discuss this matter with the other handmaidens, because she already had a mentor.

Neither did she just use her experience of having been married to get Boaz's attention. Many women follow these paths tend to end up with Bozo instead of Boaz.

Boaz was able to take care of Ruth, where Bozo usually needs someone to take care of him. Boaz will approach the woman in a valued way, where Bozo thinks he is the prize.

I could go on and on, but I think you get the picture. The main thing is that you need to run from Bozo and prepare yourself for Boaz. Your mentor will help prepare you to meet your Boaz!

Do you have a Naomi in your life?

If you don't, it is of great importance that you find one. When I married my wife, she had a Naomi named Mary Katherine. She was a dear saint who is now with the Lord. But this woman helped my wife many days when I was acting like a Bozo instead of Boaz.

She helped her to stay the course and pray through issues that many couples fight through in their early years. They would talk for hours and when they finished many of the things that we were having problems with as a couple seemed to lose intensity.

This is because she helped my wife to see them differently. Mary Katherine was a big part of us getting through our first two years of marriage.

The bible says the aged women should teach the younger women. The same holds true for men, a man needs another man in his life to talk things through with him. My instruction to women is to never get involved with a man that doesn't have another man who can tell him "no", and he listen to him. It is very important for a woman to have a Naomi in this hour.

If you notice, Ruth wasn't looking for a husband. Her concern was for Naomi and it just happened to be Boaz's field that she gleaned in. Keep your focus right and God will open the eyes of the man who will find you. When he does instead of being excited about the attention you receive discuss the matter with you mentor. If you are already married, before discussing potential problems with your spouse have a talk with your mentor, it will help you approach the issue right.

The next question is, whose Naomi are you?

There are so many young women who have no clue about what it means to be valued as a woman. These women need the correct guidance.

They are watching entertainers and movies to get their values. They are not willing to listen to their parents because they are the enemy in their minds.

These women need someone they can trust who will help give them to develop a balanced view of life. Make yourself available to a Ruth (young woman in need of guidance) and watch her life blossom.

Ruth does marry Boaz, and out of this marriage we get the divine lineage.

So Boaz took Ruth, and she was his wife: and when he went in unto her, the LORD gave her conception, and she bare a son. And the women said unto Naomi, Blessed be the LORD, which hath not left thee this day without a kinsman, that his name may be famous in Israel. And he shall be unto thee a restorer of thy life, and a nourisher of thine old age: for thy daughter in law, which loveth thee, which is better to thee than seven sons, hath born him. And Naomi took the child, and laid it in her bosom, and became nurse unto it. And the women her neighbours gave it a name, saying, There is a son born to Naomi; and they called his name Obed: he is the father of Jesse, the father of David. Ruth 4:14-17

And it is Jesus who is called David's greater son. Without the guidance of Naomi, Jesus would have needed another birth line and that would have changed more things than we have time to discuss here.

Because Ruth had Naomi, we can now say we have a Savior!

The Summary

In the beginning, we discussed that God created man and woman to rule over the works of His hands. They were given the ability to rule ("radah" in Hebrew) over the things that would submit freely, and the added ability to subdue, or "kabash" the things that would be unruly.

After giving the man and woman this dominion, God created the man in the natural sense. He came down and fashioned the man from the clay, breathed into his nostrils the breath of life, and man became a living soul.

Man is placed in the Garden of Eden to dress it and to protect it. The dressing of the Garden had to do with worship more than work since there was nothing that needed any work. And if Adam was working in the Garden, how could it be considered a part of the punishment that God handed down once the disobedience occurs?

Adam dressed in worship the place where God came down to commune with him. In the same way, it is the position of the man to dress his dwelling place before he is joined with a wife. One of the first questions a woman should ask a man is, "Can you tell me about your time worshipping God?" or, "What was the last thing He gave you in this relationship?"

It was Adam's worshipping lifestyle that prompts God to make the decision to bring his wife on the scene.
The woman was created to join with the man in true worship, which no other creature on the earth could accomplish. She was also called to be his "helpmeet" and not his helpmate. The helpmeet is one who is out in front announcing the vision and purpose of the union. When a woman takes this position, she is protected and can function from a place authority with boldness.

Therefore, she is not behind the man making him great; he is behind her making her great, which makes both of them great. The church is called the bride of Christ, but isn't responsible for making Jesus great. Jesus backs the church to accomplish what He did and even greater.

When a husband and wife function in this manner, their union pleases the Lord and causes their habitation to be dressed for His blessings.

The woman was created to join the man, but wasn't created in the same manner as the man. God took the side of the man and made the woman. In essence, the woman wasn't made from dirt but from the man so that he would value her since she was bones of his bones and flesh of his flesh.

This wasn't another being added to the equation but the same being increased. Man was the first human on earth to give birth to another human, and she was called "Woman!"

Adam recognized just how valuable the woman was in design and function, but clearly Adam didn't use her title to communicate with her. Genesis 5 instructs that their name was Adam when they were created.

Mr. and Mrs. Adam dwelt in the Garden and worshipped as one because they were one. When God came down in the cool of the day and called Adam, they both came. There was one man with one identity dwelling in the Garden and serving God!

Creation was an awesome thing but it wasn't complete until the woman was created. We could say that God saved the best for last, and that Adam was extremely grateful. God placed value upon the woman that Adam fully embraced and sought to protect. When a woman devalues her life for male companionship, she destroys all that God did in valuing her.

She is in essence saying that God should have just made her from the dirt in the way He did the man. I have talked with many women about the different way society views them against their male counterparts. My five daughters have all asked me at some point why it is that they have to act, dress and/or present themselves differently than the young men with whom they grew up.

The fact that they were created from flesh and bone and not dirt requires a different attitude and positioning. Also, because they represent me as their father to the world, they should present themselves in a way that shows that I have raised and value them so much that they know who they are, and will not lower their standard for anyone.

New statistics gathered by Ohio State University indicate that men think about sex between10 and 19 times daily on average. The long standing statistic of thinking about sex every seven seconds has been proven to be overstated.

The research proves that men think about sex more than women but these thoughts are on par with thoughts about food and sleep. Sex is a big motivation for men in a relationship and God wanted it to be that way.

The design was for the man to cleave to the wife that God gave him. When women allow their bodies to be used before the man has the desire to cleave, she is making a huge mistake.

God made the woman's womb so that through it, life would increase on the earth, and also give Him a way into the world if Adam failed. Adam did fail and Jesus entered the earth through the womb of Mary.

Since that time, the enemy has done everything in his power to pervert the womb and the desire of men to cleave to their wives through a host of distorted images and attitudes associated with the womb.

A woman must not release her body to a man who claims to care about her only to have a sexual encounter. He will not value whatever comes that easily!

One of the most difficult things I do is to convey to women the attitude of men. Since a woman can't begin to come close to thinking like a man, she can't believe men are that way. I've had this conversation more times than I can count and even though the woman appears to be listening, she is still holding out hope that I am wrong.

There are some things that you know men just don't seem to get about women and it is easy for you to see that. Why is it so difficult for women to understand that men think in ways that are different from women?

Believe me, when it comes to sex, men and women think much differently about the subject. For this reason, it is important to have a man in your life to discuss the matter with that will not try to use the situation for his own advantage.

Once women fully understand that God gave them more ability and pleasure in the area of sex, they will stop men from owning this part of the relationship. Sex is primarily for women, and we proved this fact from the body's physical makeup, the covenant seal and the pleasure center of the womb.

Everything in society leads us to believe that sex is designed for men. This all took place because of the fall of Adam and the fact a woman's desire is now to please her husband. This part of the curse means that her primary desires were taken from God and placed on her husband. Jesus came to remove the curse and restore the relationship that the man and woman had with God from the beginning, which allowed the woman to seek God first, with-- and not through, her husband.

Once in Jesus, she is saved from being a sex object and sex becomes the way that the couple enjoys their oneness, and the man proves to his wife he still cleaves to her in every way.

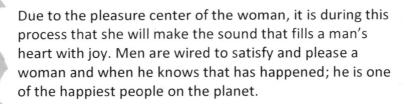

Due to the pleasure center of the woman, it is during this process that she will make the sound that fills a man's heart with joy. Men are wired to satisfy and please a woman and when he knows that has happened; he is one of the happiest people on the planet.

One of the keys to having a blessed relationship is for a woman to bring that sound of fulfillment and pleasure outside of the bedroom into her everyday life. It is not a flirting or sensual sound, but rather an "I am happy with you and honor you" sound.

Most men crave this sound and will pursue it without even knowing he is doing so. Men will visit the same store daily, passing many other stores of the same type, just to communicate with the woman who works there because she is nice and honors him.

He will wear the same shirt or tie frequently because a woman told him that it looks good on him. A woman communicating with a man using the sound will cause the toughest man's heart to melt.

Women have tried to force men to do what they want through fussing or complaining, but this sound only helps him resist the woman even more. Remember, the woman was created as a helpmeet to the man, positioned out in front in the role of announcing.

When the woman turns and faces the man, she is out of position and he must then resist her as an enemy and not as his completion. I teach the women in my church to argue from the place of vision and purpose, which is very difficult to resist because it requires the right sound.

All of this is put in motion so that the true marriage can be seen and understood, which the marriage between Christ and the Church represents.

This is the most important marriage and will always be the example for all human relationships and marriages. With society moving away from what marriage is and should be, the only thing that is unchangeable is the marriage between Christ and His church.

So that the church would clearly understand that Jesus is espoused to the church, He is following the Jewish rituals for marriage. From His coming to the earth to the way He left with a promise of returning is all perfectly in line with the marital ritual. Everything that the church is responsible for now while Jesus is away also perfectly completes its part as the waiting bride, in line with the Jewish bride.

Mankind can do whatever it wants to distort marriage and argue over who should and shouldn't be married when a true marriage between a husband and wife is happening right in front of them.

Marriage has everything to do with a covenant, and not just a contract; the two people are entering into a death agreement. The only way out of a covenant agreement is through death.

This is what Adam was speaking of once God presented his wife Mrs. Adam to him, that a man leaves his mother and father and becomes one with his wife. There is no way to divide something that has become one without destroying it. The covenant is greater than the relationship he had with his parents. This places a greater value on the wife than the parents and even the children once they arrive in the family.

Many don't embrace covenant, and enter the wedding ceremony more concerned about the wedding and all that it offers than the actual marriage. Far more planning goes into the wedding than the marriage.

For this reason, single women focus their attention on the wedding dress, the décor, and the cake more than the preparation of their lives for the one who will honor and protect their value.

Dress rehearsals for marriage take place when two people decide to live together without covenant responsibility. Society has decided that this is acceptable and even expects it to take place before the actual marriage.

One thing I know as a man is that if I can get the milk for free, you cannot convince me to buy the cow or even visit the store. Why work for what I already have? Men are hunters by nature, which means there is a great deal of effort in preparing for the kill, but once the kill takes place he stops hunting. He will mount the head on his wall and show it off. There is no need to continue hunting for what he has already caught.

Most women don't think like a hunter so they have one picture in mind and the man has a completely different picture. This is why some people have lived together for years without a marriage; the man is the one who can't understand why they should mess up a good thing by adding marriage to the equation. The woman wants security, but the man is already very secure, thinks there is no need for it, and can't understand why the woman does not see things the way he does.

Single women must value their lives so much that they will let "Mr. Right" go so that they can be loved the way God designed them to be loved!

All women must unite to learn how to love and respect themselves, and always realize that there is One who loves you with an everlasting love. This is a true and enduring love that comes from the Father.

Therefore, before allowing a man into your life you should focus on this love. Before God brought Mrs. Adam to Adam, we get the idea that God spent some time alone with her. I believe it was so that she would have an experience with God in the way Adam did in true worship alone unto the Lord.

When a woman understands this principle, she will then also look for a man who has incorporated in his life the true love relationship. He is easy to spot because his focus is on the things of God and not all of the other trappings around him.

But he still can be difficult to find so I recommend that you have a woman in your life that can help you spot this man. This woman is your Naomi; she has experience in these matters and can help you with your decision making.

You should have a Naomi and be a Naomi for someone else. Women are very relational and can get enjoyment from each other without really knowing each other, yet they can also dislike each other for no apparent reason. This has always interested me about women, how could they dislike someone from across the room. Research indicates that women have an ability to sense things that men can't which can cause them to be more careful in their dealings with people.

But I have observed the fact that sometimes the enemy is involved to cause problems between women to hinder the purposes of God. The bible teaches that the older women should be teachers of the younger women so that they won't get caught up into things that will take them away from God's call for their lives.

When women learn to help, honor, and protect each other, there will be a move on the earth that is unstoppable. The True Value conferences and seminars are designed to help women come to this understanding and began to band together for godly purposes.

Meetings are developed where women walk through the workbook and other materials that help women develop a higher level of self-esteem and purpose.

This is only the beginning of what I believe can change the way things take place in our world. Men need women who know what they want, who they are, and why they are here!

When this happens, there will be a much needed shift in the way things are seen and done by many in society. Notice that the shows that have women sitting around discussing the issues facing society don't help women to understand their value from a biblical standpoint, but rather from a liberated standpoint that is not what God intended.

These are the daughters of Eve and there need to be daughters of Sarah who will rise up to stand against this ideology without destroying their sisters. They must have a mindset of helping women realize who they are so that they can begin to fulfill their God designed destiny.

Will you join the movement?

For further information contact us at: www.betheloic.com

Understand that **You** were made to be special, therefore live your life like you are special!